D1367607

Raising Multiple Birth Children

A Parents' Survival Guide

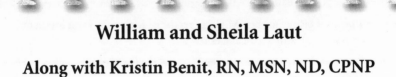

Raising Multiple Birth Children

A Parents' Survival Guide

William and Sheila Laut

Along with Kristin Benit, RN, MSN, ND, CPNP

Chandler House Press
Worcester, Massachusetts
1999

South Salem Library
15 Main Street
South Salem, NY 10590

Raising Multiple Birth Children: A Parents' Survival Guide

Copyright © 1999 by William and Sheila Laut

All rights reserved. Printed in the United States of America. No part of this book may be used or reproduced, stored or transmitted in any manner whatsoever without written permission from the Publisher, except in the case of brief quotations embodied in critical articles and reviews.

ISBN 1-886284-35-0

Library of Congress Catalog Card Number 98-89743

First Edition

ABCDEFGHIJK

Published by
Chandler House Press
335 Chandler Street
Worcester, MA 01602
USA

Book Design: Bookmakers

Cover Design: Marshall Henrichs

Cover Photos: LeRoy Dierker, M.D., Director of Maternal-Fetal Medicine, Cleveland MetroHealth Medical Center

Chandler House Press books are available at special discounts for bulk purchases. For more information about how to arrange such purchases, please contact Chandler House Press, 335 Chandler Street, Worcester, MA 01602, or call (800) 642-6657, or fax (508) 756-9425, or find us on the World Wide Web at www.chandlerhousepress.com.

Chandler House Press books are distributed to the trade by
National Book Network, Inc.
4720 Boston Way
Lanham, MD 20706
(800) 462-6420

South Salem Library
15 Main Street
South Salem, NY 10590

Dedication

To our Great Aunt Lucille, who stormed the Heavens with prayer for a safe arrival of our three angels

To my mother, Alice, who would have covered the Earth in her pride as the grandmother of our children

And to our children who have taught us so much

Contents

Foreword

The New Culture of Multiples

Years ago, large extended families were the norm. It was not uncommon, as recently as the fifties and sixties, to have a family of five, six, seven, or more. Trends changed as we entered the seventies. We became environmentally aware, we focused on personal health and exercise, and we became a little more socially conscious. We read books like *The Population Bomb,* and soon census indicators told us that families had an average of 2.2 children. (We often wondered what the .2 child would look like, but we were mainstream and went along with it.)

Today, birth rates have changed again. A *new* population explosion has occurred, but this time in a *very* different way. As a result of women choosing to have children later in life and the growing use of assisted reproduction, an unprecedented increase in the number of multiple births has occurred. A new version of the larger family has arrived, but this time, all of the children are being born at once!

A new culture of multiple birth children is growing.

Our Story

It wasn't until our babies were born that we truly understood the reality of our situation. In spite of all our preparation and planning, we were overwhelmed, overcome, and literally outnumbered! Never in our wildest dreams had we imaged the challenges of raising multiples.

We immediately began a frantic search to read anything and everything we could on the subject of raising multiples—*anything* we could get our hands on. We needed help and we needed it badly. We invented things along the way, and if we were lucky they worked. We stumbled through the sleepless nights *working harder and not smarter*—too busy with our noses to the grindstone and too exhausted to know the difference. Surely, others had raised multiples and lived to write about it. But where was it? The information we did find was scattered and fragmented. We found snippets and articles tucked away in magazines and on TV shows—of course, *Oprah*. Nevertheless, sensationalism prevailed and multiple birth families were addressed with wonder—"*Isn't it amazing?*" "*Can you imagine?*"

Where were the blueprints for the real issues and challenges families face when trying to fulfill the all-consuming demands of raising multiples?

Parenting is the most important job in the world. With multiples, the work becomes exponential! So we went to work to create this book to *help you* by bringing together a collection of firsthand knowledge, tips, techniques, and coping strategies from other parents of multiples who have walked in your shoes. We reached out to the nation and pulled together real-life experiences from parents of multiples to present the demands and rewards of their all-important work.

This book *is for you and your family*. Take advantage of the experiences of these multiple birth families: what works, what doesn't, and the funny little paradoxes that present themselves along the way. Our message to you is that your first few years as parents of multiples do not have to be a brutal blur. Raising multiples requires work, really hard work—maybe the hardest work you'll ever do—but with good planning, organization, lots of flexibility, and a sense of humor, raising your children can be some of the *best years of your life!*

Acknowledgments

To all of our family members who have helped us along each step of the way, especially Mom and Dad, for providing such excellent role models. To Linda Hubbard, whose creative and organizational talent put us on track. To Jennifer Goguen, whose keen eye for design and structure helped us package our message. To Tony Parinello, for his guidance and inspiration. To all the parents of multiples whose contributions have helped make this book possible. And to God, for his invisible hand in making everything possible—most of all, our beautiful children.

Chapter One

Congratulations, and Fasten Your Seat Belt!

"You're Kidding... Right?"

There are moments in the lives of all human beings—moments that stand out and remain fixed in our memories with extraordinary brilliance and detail. We look back on those moments and recognize them as turning points in our lives. For the parents of multiples, there is one unforgettable moment that changes their lives forever.

He said:	"What do you mean…and there's a brother or sister over there?"
She said:	"What? Where? "
He said:	"Triplets, Honey! Triplets!"
She said:	*"Turn off the sonogram! Turn it off!"*
She said:	"Oh my God."
He said:	"It's gonna be all right."
She said:	"What?"
He said:	"That's fantastic!!"

She:	Panicked.
He:	Saw dollar signs.
We:	Cried and laughed at the same time and kept on saying, *"Oh my God,"* over and over again.

Finding out that you are expecting multiples can literally take your breath away. Hearing the news brings a rush of mixed emotions surging through your mind and body like an electrical current. Emotions like pride, joy, panic, and shock, to name just a few, are accompanied by an ocean of tears and beaming smiles you can't wipe off your face. In the end, it's just awe.

Years later, we still can't believe it.

HOW IN THE WORLD ARE WE GOING TO MANAGE?

In the wake of that first wave of emotion will likely come lots of questions. You and your partner will undoubtedly struggle with questions like: *"Can my body carry more than one baby? Will I go full term and if not, how premature will they be? How will we ever afford this? Do we **really** have to buy a minivan? A bigger house? What about everything else going on in our lives? What about our other children? Will our lifestyle change forever?"*

The answers to these questions are as different as the personalities and life circumstances of those who ask them. We can answer only one of them with any certainty.

TIP!

YES. Your lifestyle will change. Forever!

There is a tremendous amount of excitement and attention that goes along with carrying multiples. This can often undermine the reality of what is in store for you and your partner and the enormous adjustments you will need to make in your lives. Consciously thinking through some of the more important issues *now* will help you stay in control later, when most of your energy will be devoted to the immediate demands of the babies.

How Do I Stay in Control?— Health Care Choices

BE AN ACTIVE PARTICIPANT IN YOUR HEALTH CARE

Multiple pregnancies pose increased risks for you and the babies, so you will want to build a first-class health care team to help you through the experience. The most important people on that team are you and your partner. The role of the health care professionals is to provide expertise, information, and support that will enable you to make informed, confident decisions about your physical and emotional health. The number one coping strategy is to be an active participant in your health care. Your questions will be endless and your quest for answers will be insatiable.

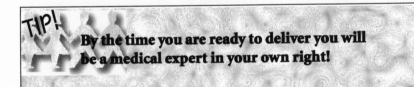

TIP! **By the time you are ready to deliver you will be a medical expert in your own right!**

YOU HAVE CHOICES

First and foremost, select a qualified physician—someone you *like and trust.* Your physician should be someone you can talk openly with. A good relationship with your doctor is imperative because you and your partner can count on seeing a lot of him or her. Pregnancies involving multiples require more doctor's visits, countless rounds of ultrasounds, fetal and uterine monitoring, lots of false alarms, and other procedures too numerous to list, which are not routine during singleton pregnancies.

Just because you need a high-risk doctor does not mean you don't have a choice. Ask for several referrals from your general obstetrician–gynecologist (OB–GYN), your fertility specialist, and other mothers of multiples in your community.

> ## TIP!
> **We saw three high-risk OBs before we found our partner of choice.**

LOOK FOR A LEVEL 3 MEDICAL FACILITY

Just as important as an excellent OB is the medical facility he or she is associated with and in which you will deliver. The National Center of Health Statistics reported that 91.6 percent of all triplets are born preterm, and 13.4 percent were born at the *extremely* preterm gestational age of less than 28 weeks.* A Level 3 Neonatal Intensive Care Unit (NICU) is ranked the highest and is best equipped to handle the critical special needs of preemies. With the average gestational age of triplets only 32 completed weeks,* it is critical to align yourself with a doctor associated with a Level 3 NICU.

Vital and Health Statistics from the Centers for Disease Control and Prevention/ National Center for Health Statistics, 1997.

TOUR THE NICU!

Most hospitals do not provide a NICU tour for expectant mothers. You will likely have to call ahead and ask to see the unit or ask your doctor to get clearance for you. This will minimize the shock of seeing such tiny little helpless babies connected to tubes, wires, devices, and monitors that your children's lives may possibly depend on. The NICU is filled with technical jargon and sophisticated equipment that can be very intimidating and frightening if you have had no exposure to it. Talk to the neonatologists and familiarize yourself with various scenarios. We were able to see the unit while Sheila was on bedrest in the hospital. Take a proactive and assertive approach to having your questions answered.

QUESTIONS FOR THE DOC

Since you and your doctor are going to be seeing a lot of each other, keep a special pad of paper nearby to capture your questions and concerns. Sheila kept paper and pen at the side of the bed where she spent most of her time.

In your condition, your memory is likely to be in a state of brain scatter, so jot down _all_ of your questions, large and small, as they come to mind. On your next visit, leave your ego at home and ask each question on your list!

Believe it, answers and information will keep your mind from all the pacing *"what ifs…"* and you and your partner will sleep better. Besides providing reassurance and peace of mind, the information will educate you and add even *more* excitement to the pregnancy. The more you understand what is happening, the greater sense of control you will experience about the important decisions that are being made about you and your babies' health.

It Cannot Be Compared

You may be tempted to compare your pregnancy to a singleton pregnancy. Don't. A multiple pregnancy is worlds apart from that of a singleton. *Everything about it is exaggerated.* There are multiple health risks and potential complications both for mother and babies. Premature labor is a constant threat. Hormones surge right off the charts making you a delight to live with, yet impossible to deal with. The impending joy and anxiety are profound and power-packed with emotions.

With a multiple pregnancy, everything gets bigger—your body, your risks, your excitement, your anticipation, your worries... and your expenses!

The physical fatigue alone can be overwhelming during the first trimester.

> *"Something was really up. My wife would lie on the living room floor, overcome with exhaustion and fatigue. Wild horses couldn't drag her away."*
>
> **—Bill, Before We Knew**

Think about what is happening biologically. Your body is going through an amazing process of rapidly building magnificent multiple life support systems—each with his or her own little beating heart and soul! Your heart is working hard to pump what will eventually become an enormous increase in blood volume running through your own veins.

TIP!

For twins you can expect a 75% increase in your blood volume. For triplets a whopping 100% increase, and for quads, 100% plus!

This takes work! It is no different than climbing a mountain or running a marathon. No wonder you're tired!

Announcing Your Pregnancy at Work

The approach you take to announcing your pregnancy at work will depend upon the type of work you do, your health risks, and how you feel about dealing with the wave of questions you will get once you announce it. Here are a couple of approaches to consider:

- Wait to announce until after your first trimester—anything can go wrong.
- If you work in a non-office environment—in a factory, for example, where you may be exposed to hazardous conditions—you may want to announce your pregnancy sooner.
- Tell them right away! Most parents tell us they were too excited and told the world at every opportunity!

Whenever you decide to announce it, be prepared for the well-wishers, the doom and gloom skeptics, and the avalanche of questions that will follow.

"I was very fortunate that I worked for a company that not only supported mothers and mothers-to-be... it applauded them!"

—DB, Puxico, Mo.

"I told my boss and then e-mailed the rest of the department! I wanted everyone to know and pray for me and my husband."

—JB, Birmingham, Ala.

Hope for a Flexible Employer

If you have announced your pregnancy at work, your employer may be supportive and flexible and allow you to take some time during the day to recharge your batteries.

Some women have arranged to telecommute, managing their work via their laptop and telephone. This is a great way to keep the money rolling in and keep up your mental activity while taking the best possible care of yourself.

"After lunch, I would just sit in my office, eyes closed, let my telephone calls roll to voice mail and hope that no one would enter my work area as I would catch my breath."

—Sheila

How Long Should I Continue to Work?

This can be a balancing act because, like most families, you need the income but you also want to do everything possible during your pregnancy to insure a positive outcome.

TIP!

Follow your doctor's advice, listen to your body, and do what is best for your babies.

Some women report they stopped working and got off their feet immediately because the risk wasn't worth it; others continued to work into their twenty-sixth week or longer.

"My Goodness, I'm as Big as a Tank"— Enjoying Your Pregnancy

Being pregnant with multiples will have its ups and downs, but with the right attitude, it can be a fantastic, unforgettable experience.

Keep A Journal

Keeping a journal during this incredible time will help both of you to deal with the emotional issues surrounding the pregnancy by allowing you to express your worries, fears, and excitement. It will also provide a cherished history of the many adjustments you make and hurdles you cross over during this momentous journey.

Log everything—the good, the bad, and the ugly. Record how proud you are. Write about the days of waiting and anticipation. Include the current events of the day and age.

"I was active in my job and even traveled by air to other cities and was doing fine. At the end of each day I was always exhausted and would come home and immediately put on my pajamas, even if it was only five o'clock in the afternoon. There was no medical reason why I could not work, but as I got bigger and bigger, I began moving slower and slower. I finally said, 'Uncle'!"

—Sheila in Slow Motion

"One thing I wish I had done was to keep a diary throughout the pregnancy. I did not do this, and many details are blurred in all the excitement of the time."

—DB, Puxico, Mo.

> **TIP!**
>
> **Log the ups and downs—literally—like when chronic indigestion forced you to sleep sitting up, because no stomach in the world has real estate priority over your ever-expanding babies!**

Include the shortness of breath and the chronic itching of your belly. Record the funny and not so funny times when you had difficulty walking, sleeping, and sometimes just thinking. All of these experiences will soon be just a memory. In years to come, as you look back on this extraordinary time in your life, you will be glad you kept a journal.

Each time we reread our journals, we relive the sense of power, pride, and gratitude Sheila felt when she wrote:

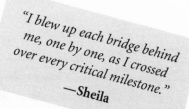

"I blew up each bridge behind me, one by one, as I crossed over every critical milestone."
—Sheila

SCRAPBOOKS

Keeping a scrapbook during the pregnancy is another way to remember this amazing experience. When you look back, you will reminisce and enjoy.

❖ Take lots of photos at various stages of pregnancy, showing off your magnificent progress.

❖ Be sure to date the photos immediately after they are developed or hold up a sign in the photo telling how many weeks along you are.

❖ Include printouts of your sonograms showing "*Baby A*," "*Baby B*," "*Baby C*," "*Baby D*."

❖ Be proud! Get out the measuring tape and measure your rotund body weekly.

❖ Keep cards from well-wishers, clippings from local newspapers, even a napkin from your favorite take-out restaurant.

❖ Hold on to the calendar that you lived by, to remind yourselves of all the milestone dates and doctor's appointments.

TIP!

Years from now, when your babies are old enough to look at the scrapbook with you, they will be fascinated by this glimpse into their earliest beginnings.

Stretched to the Breaking Point— Coping with the "What Ifs"

While all pregnancies are marked by mood swings, a woman carrying more than one child can be downright difficult to live with. The vision of a calm, serene woman with child who "has the glow" is not likely to apply to multiple birth pregnancies.

While it is a time of excitement and anticipation, high-risk multiple pregnancies are also plagued by worry and deep concern. Time is spent counting the days, the weeks. Home uterine monitoring and efforts to ward off preterm labor are constant reminders of the risks. Much time is spent reading everything you can get your hands on that relates to multiple pregnancies, which often reveals hard cold facts about real things that can go wrong. There is a tendency to mentally construct worst-case scenarios.

"She's hot, she's tired, and she wants to go shopping. Leave her alone."

—Richard Laut, my father-in-law's words to my husband

"I had a star on my calendar for each week and a big "WE MADE IT!" after reaching 32 weeks. I delivered at 34+ weeks."

—KD, N. Olmstead, Ohio

> **TIP!**
>
> **While saturated with elevated hormones, we tend to focus on numbers and percentages, charts, and benchmarks. It can make you nuts!**
>
> **Stay aware of your own physical and mental health. Listen to your doctor and listen to your body.**

"My fears dealt primarily with the health of the children. I had never seen triplets, let alone known anyone with three or more. The best way to deal with those fears was to talk to all the doctors involved and get the WHOLE truth. I wanted to know the best- and worst-case scenarios and everything in between."

—DB, Puxico, Mo.

"We knew we needed to be ready for anything. We tried to educate ourselves about what to look for and I tried to pay great attention to everything my body was telling me. It was a mind game I was going to win—worrying was not going to do me any good."

—NJ, Macedonia, Ohio

"What Am I Going to Wear?"

You and your maternity clothes will get to know each other very well. You'll start wearing them sooner, and stay in them longer; even after the birth as your body tries to reclaim its original pre-pregnancy shape.

❖ Buy comfortable items larger than you think you'll need, as you are likely to outgrow standard maternity clothes such as pants and skirts. Expansive tent style dresses work best because they are versatile, comfortable, look pretty decent, and adapt along the way to your ever-expanding body.

✖ If you're not on a budget now, you soon will be! Try the upscale resale shops for great deals! These shops usually have high standards and only accept high quality "gently worn" garments in very good to excellent condition. They often have a small selection of upscale maternity clothes. Now you can look great for a fraction of the cost!

✖ Outlet stores are great sources for good deals. You can also borrow clothes from others. You might be surprised at how eager people will be to help!

Move Over and Let Someone Else Take Over!

One of the most important lessons you can learn during your pregnancy is that it is OK to let other people help you. In modern western culture, where independence and self-sufficiency are considered primary virtues, this is both a difficult and valuable lesson to learn.

"At 31 weeks, I was humorously referring to myself as 'Large Marge.' I could hardly waddle from one end of the house to the other, let alone go out shopping. I had cabin fever so bad, I <u>insisted</u> that my husband take me along for the ride to Kmart. Yes, Kmart. I was willing to go anywhere. I called ahead and asked if they had one of those electric carts for the handicapped. YES! I was going cruisin' in Kmart! Well, being an inexperienced driver of these little go-carts, I banged into every display case in my path and knocked over a myriad of aisle end caps filled with Christmas merchandise. (It's <u>hard</u> to figure out which button goes forward and which one goes in reverse!) Bill, so embarrassed, insisted I go back to the car and wait. Pedal to the metal, I zoomed down the main aisle toward the store's exit. I could hear a faint voice behind me, 'Ma'am... Ma'am... Excuse me, ma'am... HEY YOU! in the electric cart!' I was dragging an entire dried flower arrangement behind me. Humbled, I waddled back to the car and that was the last time I went out in public until after the babies were born."

—Sheila in Full Bloom

TIP! If accepting help doesn't come easily to you, circumstances will be your teacher, and eventually you'll learn to accept help with humor and grace. After the babies arrive, it's a lesson you'll be glad you learned.

OB Wannabes— Managing Unwanted Advice

Like it or not, the OB wannabes go with the territory. Unsolicited advice on how to stay pregnant will come to you from all angles. You will hear everything from home-spun remedies, family traditions, and ethnic customs to sound, practical advice.

The overly opinionated meddlers will offer you advice on what to eat, how to sleep, how to sit, why you should breastfeed, why you don't need to... and so on. They are generally well-meaning, so take it in stride.

"At first, when you want to go to the store, you just get in the car and go. Then you reach a point in your pregnancy when you don't fit behind the wheel of a car, so you let others do the driving. Then you reach a new point, when you stay in the car while your driver runs into the stores for you. Eventually, it gets to be too much to get out at all, and you just send someone else."

—Triplet Mom, San Francisco, Calif.

TIP! Besides, this is good practice for what's in store for you once the babies arrive!

SET BOUNDARIES

A tactic that works most of the time is to politely thank your eager advice giver, tell them you have already made a decision

on that particular topic, and gently change the subject by asking them a question:

❖ "Thanks for your tip, we'll keep it in mind, so tell me, how old are your children?"

❖ "Thanks for your advice, we've already talked that one through, so tell me, what do you think of those Chicago Bulls?"

"During my last final weeks of pregnancy I received phone calls daily from everyone asking the same questions over and over, 'How are you coming along?' 'Any new developments?' 'What is the doctor saying?' I finally had to politely tell them that if they were going to call me, please call me to talk to me and to lighten up on the back-to-back questions."

—NJ, Macedonia, Ohio

"I loved being on bedrest, but I felt sorry for my husband who had to do all the added work."

—GW, Fairfield, Calif.

"I enjoyed coming home from work every day and waiting on my very pregnant wife. It was everything that everyone who had gone through this experience had talked about and more. It made me feel like I was part of the pregnancy."

—Bill

The excitement and anticipation from caring family and friends seems to build as the pregnancy nears its end. This anticipation reveals itself in the form of never-ending questions about you and the babies' health. In your heightened emotional state, this can wear on you as you wait... and wait... for the babies to arrive.

"Laying Around Is Hard Work!"— What to Do While on Bedrest

Pregnancies involving multiples require the expectant mother to be on bedrest for weeks or even months. Once you and your doctor make the decision that it is time for bedrest, the entire family will have to make significant adjustments.

TIP!

Everyone is affected, no one is spared, not even the family pet!

Someone must take over all the activities involved in managing the home. This includes cooking, cleaning, shopping, caring for older children, and waiting on the mom-to-be. These tasks often fall to the man of the house and the older children. It helps if everyone in the family can be patient and learn to relax their standards a bit about what constitutes a clean house or a home-cooked meal.

Bedrest is surprisingly hard work for the mother-to-be as well! In addition to physical discomfort, the boredom and isolation can build and lead to a major case of cabin fever. Yes, we know, you were going to knit those booties, play duplicate bridge on the Internet, and write that book you always wanted to write while on bedrest. Well, it requires a conscious act of will to exchange independence and control for the helplessness and stress that comes while waiting as your babies grow.

Mom's bedrest can profoundly affect the children in the family, too. It can be difficult, especially for toddlers, to understand why Mommy can't be up and about. Accept the fact that you will not be able to care for them alone. Arrange for a relative or hire a sitter to care for your toddler(s) and to do light housekeeping while Dad is at work.

> "I was constantly tired.... I lived in a recliner."
> —GW, Fairfield, Calif.

TIP! Turn this situation into a great opportunity to spend quality time together, allowing you to strengthen the bond and ease their adjustment to the babies who are on their way.

> "I had a wonderful neighbor who took care of my two- and three- year-olds during the day, and my husband came home from work and took care of the kids, dinner, and laundry at night...(my husband had to learn to read the labels!)"
> —GW, Fairfield, Calif.

Share quiet times together: reading, singing songs, playing games, checking homework, watching videos, or just talking.

Keep a sense of humor and keep talking to one another. Occasional words of encouragement or appreciation can go a long way.

As for the family pet, they usually get the best end of the deal because they have someone to snuggle with all day long, and one that can fetch is a genuine asset.

"JABBA THE HUTT" IN STYLE

From the right perspective, a period of bedrest can be viewed as a special time filled with snacks and naps and being waited on. One thing is for sure, enjoy it now, because once the babies are born it may be years before you will experience this kind of peace and quiet.

So, make the best of it. Here are a few tips to help you enjoy your final stages of pregnancy and to stay as comfortable as possible.

SLEEP!

Sleep eighteen hours a day and eat during the other six.

READ!

Line up all those books you were "going to read" and read them! Read everything.

SURF!

There are tons of web sites on the Internet. Just type in "twins, multiples, supertwins" and you'll be on for hours!

CHAT!

Log onto a chat room and you will find tons of people out there who are in your condition, coping with the same or similar concerns. This is a fun way to pass the time, and you'll be reminded that you're not alone.

"Unfortunately, I learned that the things I normally enjoyed doing that could be done on bedrest (especially reading) were no longer enjoyable; because that's all I COULD do, it was no longer a treat for me."

—DB, Puxico, Mo.

CALL!

When you are at your lowest, refresh your perspective by calling other parents of multiples. Once again, this will bring into perspective that you are not alone.

WRITE!

Catch up on all those piles on your desk.

"I spent an enormous amount of time writing letters and addressing and stuffing envelopes, and then going through the responses. I also had a lot of insurance paperwork to sort and follow up on, so I did that as well."

—DB, Puxico, Mo.

WATCH!

Move the TV and VCR into the bedroom and rent lots of movies. The classics, mysteries, comedies—all your favorites. You and your partner may also want to watch a video on a Cesarean birth so you'll know what could be in store for you.

LISTEN!

Tune in to your favorite music station or radio talk show. Audio books are also very engaging.

> "All I did was sleep and eat and focus on the health of my babies. I looked forward to every medical appointment. They became the highlight of each week—I even put on make-up! I couldn't focus on anything else."
>
> —Sheila

> "I broke down and started watching the trash TV talk shows. My husband would come home from work and 'bust me!'"
>
> —Confessions of a Triplet Mother-To-Be

EAT!

Make every bite count! Carrying multiples requires good nutrition for everyone, which means a higher intake of nutrients and calories and higher weight gain. Prepare a list of recommended foods and easy meal ideas before you become immobilized.

Eating can become difficult as the babies invade the space that once was occupied by your stomach. Keep plenty of snacks at the bedside so you can nibble a little at a time. Listen to your doctor and follow the recommended eating plan.

SOOTHE!

Keep your favorite bottle of lotion or cream for your over-ripe tummy and bottles of Tums at your bedside for the *ever-present indigestion.*

COUNT!

Check off the weeks and days of your magnificent progress.

SEPARATE!

Sleep in a separate bed from your partner. You will be up and down all night from the unmerciful indigestion and back and forth to the bathroom from the relentless pressure on your bladder. Simply rolling over is a multi-step procedure that involves

> "I listened to books on tape after my vision became blurred from the Mag- Sulfate."
>
> —SN, New Philadelphia, Ohio

lots of bracing and groaning. The time is coming when neither one of you will get any sleep. He might as well get a good night's rest while he can.

MONITOR: "HONEY, IT'S THE MONITORING POLICE ON THE PHONE AGAIN"

At some point, your doctor may recommend home uterine monitoring. Home uterine monitoring can detect early patterns of contractions that a woman may not even know she is having. A belt worn low across your belly has a detection sensor that measures contractions. At the end of each monitoring session, you simply insert the sensor into a transmitting cradle that connects to your telephone. The data collected on the

> "Our goals were twenty weeks, twenty-four weeks, twenty-eight weeks, then every two weeks. Once we hit thirty-four weeks it was a different story. I wanted them out!! We made it to thirty-five and one-half weeks."
>
> —NJ, Macedonia, Ohio

sensor is transmitted over your telephone line to a monitoring center. A nurse calls after each session with a status report that indicates if your contractions are starting to build. They then advise you of a tactical plan to ward off what could tailspin into preterm labor. That's the good part.

The bad part is it is difficult for any woman in this condition to *lay still* for an hour at a time, several times a day, during monitoring sessions. Second, sometimes the contraction episodes are false alarms that result in expensive and inconvenient trips to the hospital. Third, the frequent telephone calls from the monitoring station after each monitoring session wear thin quickly and soon you know before you even pick up the phone that it is the monitoring staff calling. It's a necessary evil. The longer you can carry the babies, the better their chances for a healthy outcome, and home monitoring has helped countless women stay pregnant longer.

Some insurance companies will pay all of the costs, probably recognizing that home monitoring is less expensive than the costs associated with caring for premature babies in the NICU whose preterm birth could have been prevented if contractions had been detected sooner.

Chapter Two

"Time to Feather Your Nest"
A Guide to What You Will Need

"We've Got Plenty of Time!"—
Things You Must Do Before Delivery

Some days it will seem like you've been pregnant forever, and yet you'll tell yourself that you still have plenty of time before the babies arrive. Multiples have a way of arriving sooner than you expect and once they're here, you will feel like you're running up the down escalator! Don't make the mistake of waiting until the last minute to prepare. Prep now, because once the babies arrive your time will no longer be your own.

BEGIN BY ASKING YOURSELF SOME SERIOUS QUESTIONS

❈ What will our family be like? Talk openly with your family about how you perceive the family unit changing once the babies arrive. If the family is just you and your partner, there may be mixed emotions about plans going down the drain and putting your life on hold. Talk about it now, while you have the time, and agree to help each other work through the changes.

- How will we make time for our older children, and what impact will the babies have on their lives?
- How will we feed these babies seven, eight, nine times a day, twenty-four hours a day, and who will help us care for them when we need to sleep?
- Who will help with the general household tasks of laundry, shopping, and cleaning?
- What baby equipment and supplies do we need, and how will we afford them?
- How can we organize the house and the nursery to make caring for the babies more efficient?
- What is covered by my medical insurance? Sooner or later, I may become disabled. Do I have disability insurance?
- How much maternity time will I have? Do we have paternity leave?
- Do we want to take advantage of the Family Leave Act of 1993, which requires employers with fifty employees or more to allow up to twelve weeks of unpaid leave per year for childbirth? The Act states that your employer must continue your medical benefits during your leave of absence and that they cannot be eliminated. It also states that upon return after twelve weeks, your employer must provide you with a comparable job. Both men and women are covered under this Act. (See Chapter 14 on where to turn for more information.)
- What adjustments do we have to make in order to live on one income?
- Do I have my partner's cell phone and/or pager number—how can I reach him in an emergency?
- What will we name all these babies?

Answers to the Riddles!

Now that you've started to ponder what tomorrow might bring, it's time to start looking for some answers. One of the main reasons we wrote this book was to share some of the ways we, and other parents of multiples, have found to overcome the challenges of raising multiples (and to point out some things that didn't work!).

TIP!

You don't have to learn it all from scratch!

You, too, will learn as you go and will find ways that work for you. We hope that you will get involved in one of the many support groups for parents of multiples and will pass on your experiences and support to others. Turn to the end of this chapter for a list of support groups.

"Six of These... A Dozen of Those..." — Equipment Needed for Multiples

There is a *huge* market out there for baby equipment and supplies. Even Toys R Us has opened up Babies R Us stores across the nation. Unless you are loaded with dough, the baby stuff you will need can put a big dent in your wallet. So we have created a checklist with three categories: "Must Have," "Nice To Have," and "Need." Write your requirements in the "Need" column. Below we have listed the equipment needed for triplets based on our own experience, but if you have twins or other multiples, adjust the quantities accordingly.

CHECKLIST (for triplets)

EQUIPMENT	MUST HAVE	NICE TO HAVE	NEED
Cribs	3	3	
Mattresses	3	3	
Crib Sheets	6	9	
Crib Bumpers	3	3	
Plastic Mattress Covers	3	3	
Receiving Blankets	15	18	
Sleeping Blankets	9	12	
Mobiles	3	3	

CHECKLIST (for triplets) (Continued)

EQUIPMENT	MUST HAVE	NICE TO HAVE	NEED
Busy Boxes	3	3	
Sleepers with snaps (easier access than buttons!)	12	15	
Bassinets	0	3	
Infant Car Seats	3	3	
Infant Headrests	3	9	
Child Car Seats	3	6	
Changing Tables	1	2	
Reclining High Chairs	3	3	
Dishwasher Cap and Nipple Holder	1	1	
Bibs—Velcro or snaps— no ties!	12	18	
Old-fashioned Cloth Diapers for burping and spills	15	21	
Spill-proof Cups	6	9	
Plastic Cereal Bowls	9	18	
Starter Spoons Sets	3	6	
Laundry Baskets	6	9	
Single Vibrating Bouncy Seats	2	3	
Twin Bouncy Seat	1	1	
Playpens	1	3	
Swings	3	3	
Booster Seats	3	3	
Connectable Six-Panel Play-yards	2	4	
Safety Gates	As many as required	As many as required	

CHECKLIST (for triplets) (Continued)

EQUIPMENT	MUST HAVE	NICE TO HAVE	NEED
Walker/Saucers	2	3	
Baby Jump-ups	1	3	
Activity Gyms	1	3	
Large Diaper Pails	1	2	
Large Diaper Bags	1	2	
Backpacks	1	2	
Fanny Packs	1	2	
Snugglies	0	2	
Portable Cribs	3	3	
Triplet Stroller	1	1	
Double Stroller—one that is fast and easy to set up and collapse	1	1	
Single Umbrella Stroller	1	2	
Instant Ear Thermometer	1	1	
Gliding Rocking Chair	1	2	
"The Boss" LITE Cordless Sweeper by Eureka	0	1	
Little Tikes plastic picnic table	1	1	
Food Processor	0	1	
Cordless Phone	1	3	
Video Camera	1	1	
Minivan	1	1	
Mini Shop Vacuum	1	1	
Earplugs	6	12	

We almost forgot diapers and bottles! Yes, diapers and bottles. You're going to need lots of them! Just look at what you can expect!

DISPOSABLE DIAPERS CHANGED IN THE *FIRST YEAR!*

Twins	4,522
Triplets	6,800*
Quadruplets	8,200*

NUMBER OF BOTTLES PREPARED IN THE *FIRST YEAR!*

Twins	3,267
Triplets	4,900*
Quadruplets	6,500*

ESTIMATED COST OF DIAPERS DURING THE *FIRST YEAR* (AVERAGE COST PER DISPOSABLE DIAPER $0.25)

Twins	$1,130
Triplets	$1,700
Quadruplets	$2,050

After the first year they will go through fewer diapers on a daily basis, but by the time they are potty trained you will have made your lifetime contribution to our nation's landfills:

Twins	12,000 diapers
Triplets	18,000 diapers
Quadruplets	24,000 diapers

* Source: MOST –Mothers of Supertwins, Inc. Annual Research and Survey Results 1987-1994.

TIP! Forget the odorless-style diaper pails. We received these as shower gifts but they are too small. You'll be emptying them on the hour! Suggest a large old-fashioned diaper pail, the kind with a foot pedal, that can take a tall kitchen plastic garbage bag. Use fabric softener sheets inside the pail to keep it smelling fresh.

MULTIPLE EVERYTHING?

You don't always have to have one of everything for each baby. For example, you do not need one baby jump-up and walker for each baby. Since not every baby will respond to them the same way at the same time, simply alternate. You can manage with just one changing table; however, having two or three changing stations scattered throughout the house will save time and steps.

WAIT!

Now, before you panic or start planning a bank heist, remember what we said about learning to let others help. Read on to learn some creative ways to gather many of the things you will need to feed, clothe, and entertain your babies.

"Yes, Virginia, There Is a Santa Claus"— Free Stuff from Manufacturers

CONTACT SYMPATHETIC COMPANIES

Many companies extend their generosity to multiple birth families. It is a good idea to call first, since they change their programs from time to time. Ask for Customer Relations and ask about their Multiple Birth Program. Most companies will require a written correspondence from you with copies of the children's birth certificates.

COMPANY	CONTACT	DESCRIPTION
Arquest (DRI Bottoms) Wal-Mart house brand	(800) 526-0914 (888) 277-8378	Register with them and receive mailers with discount coupons.
Beechnut Nutrition Corp.	(800) 523-6633	Coupons and literature; Double coupons for twins, Triple coupons for triplets. Additional savings are explained in the introductory packet they send.
Carnation Nutritional Products Division	(800) 782-7766	Receive a free baby magazine with coupons, plus instructions on how to receive additional coupons.
Carter's Co.	(888) 782-9548 William Carter Co. 1124 Carver Road Griffin, GA 30224 Attn: Multiple birth program	*Triplets or more receive free clothing—currently three snap shirts, three sleepers, three body shirts.
Drypers Corp.	(360) 693-6688 (713) 682-6848 (614) 387-1243 Drypers Corp. P.O. Box 8830 Vancouver, WA 98666-8830	*Receive coupons and vouchers.
Earth's Best Baby Food	(800) 442-4221	Mention you have multiples and receive newsletters, coupons, product information, plus free rice cereal and a feeding bowl for each child.

EvenFlo Products	(800) 233-5921 EvenFlo 1801 Commerce Dr. Piqua, OH 45356 Attn: Multiple birth program	*Receive an assortment of free items such as feeding utensils. Items sent are periodically changed, so you may receive something different.
First Years Baby Products	(800) 533-6708 1 Kiddie Drive Avon, MA 02322-1171	*Receive free baby products such as bibs and rattles.
Fisher Price	(800) 432-5437	Enroll in their family registry and receive brochures, catalogs, and coupons.
Gerber	(800) 828-9119 (800) 443-7237 Gerber Products 445 State St. Fremont, MI 4913	*Receive coupons.
H.J. Heinz	(800) 544-1847	Receive a free booklet with coupons.
Healthtex Clothing	(800) USA-BABY (800) 872-2229	Receive coupons and mailings.
JC Penney Photo	(800) 597-6453 Life Touch 11000 Viking Dr. Suite 200 Eden Prairie, MN 55344	Send a letter of request to Life Touch. If you have twins, receive two certificates, each good for a two-sheet portrait package. Receive three certificates if you have triplets.
Johnson & Johnson	(800) 526-3967 Johnson & Johnson 199 Grandview Rd. Skillman, NJ 08558	Receive a one-time mailing containing coupons and a brochure on "Baby Basics."

Kimberly Clark (Huggies)	(800) 544-1847 P.O. Box 2020 Dept. Q-M-B Neenah, WI 54957-2020	*Receive free coupons.
Lego	(800) 233-8756 www.lego.com	Receive a catalog with coupons.
Lever Brothers	(800) 598-1223 Lever Brothers 390 Park Ave. New York, NY 10022	Receive coupons for detergent and Snuggle fabric softener.
Little Me	(800) 533-5437 (301) 729-4488 Little Me P.O. Box 1742 Cumberland, MD 21502	*Triplets or higher order multiples will receive free samples of their clothing. Be sure to include weights and sizes in your request.
Little Tikes	(800) 321-0183 www.Littletikes.com Little Tikes Co. Contribution Committee 2180 Barlow Rd. P.O. Box 2277 Hudson, OH 44236-0877	*Apply before the babies are six months old and receive complimentary baby toys.
McNeil Consumer Products	(800) 962-5357 (215) 533-7000	Receive coupons and literature.
Mead Johnson Nutrition	(800) 422-2902	Enroll in their "Enfamil Family discount program" for coupons and other free gifts. Also have your doctor contact his company representative, and if his budget allows, receive a free case of formula for each baby.

Mondial	(800) 843-6430 Mondial Consumer Services Attn: Multiple Birth Program 600 Mondial Pkwy Streetsboro, OH 44241	Contact before the babies are three months old and receive a free Diaper Genie.
Novartis Consumer Health, Inc. (Triaminic)	(800) 453-5330	Join their parents club to receive coupons and their magazine with discounts on products.
Ocean Spray Cranberries, Inc.	(800) 662-3263 (508) 946-1000	Receive a booklet, "What's This Stuff" a parent's guide to picky eaters, and coupons.
One Step Ahead	(800) 274-8440	Receive a special Twins/Triplets catalog. You are eligible for a 20 percent discount on your second item and 30 percent when ordering two or more of the same item. If ordering by phone (highly recommended) they will calculate the discount for you. If ordering by mail you must calculate the discount. Be sure to include a note saying that you have twins or triplets and give their birthday.

Pets & People/Mother's Little Miracle	(310) 544-7125 Fax Birth Certificates to: (310) 544-7129 or Write: Mother's Little Helper 27520 Hawthorne Blvd., Suite 125 Rolling Hills Estates, CA 90274	*Receive a gift pack containing sample stain and odor remover, air freshener, and Absorba vomit remover.
Playtex Baby Products	(800) 222-0453 www.playtexbaby .com Playtex Baby Products Consumer Affairs Multiple Birth Program 215 College Rd. Paramus, NJ 07652	*Send a letter with your return address stating your interest in their multiple birth program and receive an introductory gift pack for each child.
Premiewear	(800) 992-8469 www.premiewear.com	Receive a free catalog.
Proctor and Gamble	(800) 543-0480 (800) 285-6064 To be added to their Diaper Mailing List: (800) 699-7916 To purchase premie diapers by the case: (800) 543-4932	*P&G will send you an envelope to return to them containing copies of birth certificates, your name, address, and phone number. They will then send you coupons for free diapers, wipes, and Dreft laundry detergent.
Ringling Brothers and Barnum and Bailey Show	P.O. Box 39845 Edina, MN 55439	Receive free ticket to use anytime during lifetime. Send child's name, address, and birth date.

Ross Laboratories	(800) 222-9546	Enroll in their Welcome Addition Club via a recording to receive formula samples and coupons.
Safe Beginnings	(800) 598-8911	When you call they will register you in their multiple birth program. Each time you order, receive discounts as follows: Twins = 15 percent Triplets = 20 percent Quads = 25 percent Note: They also have special discounts through many insurance companies, so your discount may be higher; be sure to ask.
Sassy, Inc.	(800) 345-5831	They will send an information packet to explain their program. Basically it is a buy one get one, two, or three free (Twins, Triplets, Quadruplets) program.
Spencers, Inc.	(800) 633-9111 Spencers, Inc. Attn: Quality Control P.O. Box 988 Mt. Airy, NC 27030	*Receive a letter about their company, an order form for their zip leg sleeper, and a free growth chart.

Today's Kids	(800) 258-8697 Today's Kids Consumer Services P.O. Box 207 Booneville, AR 72927	*Receive a catalog from which you may choose one free toy. (We chose a wonderful rocking horse complete with motion activated sound— very generous company).
The Wooden Soldier	(800) 375-6002	Receive a free catalog specific to multiples.
The Welcome Wagon	Check your local phone book.	They will often send a packet of coupons and vouchers for free merchandise from local merchants.
Whitehall Robins/ A-H-Robbins/Lederle (Lederle Consumer Health)	(800) 322-3129 (804) 257-2000 (800) 282-8805 Whitehall Robins Product Quality 1407 Cummings Dr. Richmond, VA 23261-6609	Receive coupons and free baby Ambesol.

* Copies of birth certificates, hospital letter, newspaper clipping, or other official proof of birth is required.

TIP!

When shopping retail, ask the store manager if they have a discount for multiples. If they don't, they may create one on the fly, or simply give you special consideration.

"Do You Want to Know What We Really Need?"—Creative Baby Shower Ideas

Relatives, friends, neighbors, co-workers, and sometimes complete strangers—it seems everyone wants to share in the excitement and wonder of multiples. We even received hand-knitted booties *all the way from Australia!* Your job is to let them know what you need and organize their efforts so they can be the most help.

TIP! **We've gathered some really great ideas for shower hosts and gift givers. You might want to put a bookmark in this section of the book, or copy out some of your favorite ideas to share with friends and relatives when they ask what you need.**

REGISTER

Register at Target, Babies R Us, Toys R Us, or any other local retailer that carries baby necessities. Include everything on your "Must Have" and "Nice To Have" lists. This is an excellent way of stating what you need and minimizing the possibility of receiving too many of one particular item. Your guests will appreciate this because it eliminates the guesswork. Keep in mind that most people *want* to help you, and this is a great way to let them participate in a meaningful and helpful way.

"Our grocer would sometime slap a 'free' sticker on a gallon of milk as we would cruise the aisles. I think it made him feel better to give than it felt for us to receive. Babies bring out the best in people!"

—RW, Chicago, Ill.

"Our local store would call us in advance to let us know when diapers and wipes were going on sale. They let us come down and go into the back room and buy cases at a time before they went out on the floor and got picked over."

—Bargain Bill

SWINGS

Hands down, this is one piece of equipment parents of multiples say they cannot do without. It is right up there with cribs, strollers, and Podee hands-free bottles.

> **TIP!** **They'll be in constant motion, all humming at different speeds, none of them keeping time with each other.**

If possible, get the battery-operated, open-access style. They are much quieter than a wind-up, and the easy access will save wear and tear on your back when lifting the babies in and out.

> **TIP!** **Important Note—Babies should always be securely fastened in their swings to avoid accidents.**

"When I learned that the battery-operated swings would swing up to 150 hours, I said, 'I'll take three!' They take up a lot of space, but if they don't, something else will. The babies can all swing together, and you will have the freedom to eat, use the bathroom, make a phone call or two, or whatever."

—Sheila Swinging Free

"For me, swings were an absolute life saver. All of mine had colic and the ONLY way they would sleep was in the swings. I had to pack the swings full of blankets because the babies were so tiny, but without them I would have lost my sanity."

—DB, Puxico, Missouri

STROLLERS

Along with swings, strollers are a must-have. Most parents tell us they prefer the in-line twin stroller rather than a side-by-side configuration. Because of its width, the side-by-side stroller is often difficult to maneuver around the tight turns often necessary indoors.

TIP!

An in-line double stroller is more practical in that it is easier to maneuver in tight spots such as grocery check-out lanes and parking lot spaces.

There are two popular manufacturers of in-line triplet strollers, Peg Perego and Runabout. If your budget is of concern, you can find these strollers second-hand.

- ✵ The best place to check with is your local multiples support group.

- ✵ Triplet Connection and MOST also sell used strollers.

- ✵ Many are available on the Internet, but the money you save buying used can be eaten up by the shipping costs.

- ✵ You will also need a single stroller.

HANDS-FREE BOTTLES—NEVER PROP A BOTTLE AGAIN!

These wonderful little inventions are another tool that parents of multiples tell us they can't live without. The hands-free bottle design enables you to accomplish simple things you could never do if you had to feed each baby by hand. By simple things, I mean scratching the itch on your nose, or reaching for a bib after a major spit up. As they

"We found it (an umbrella stroller) to be the most useful piece of equipment inside and it is now a permanent part of our living room. It's a handy place to put a baby as you move around, but the most useful part is that you can stroll one around the house while holding another, and the third is in the swing!"

—KG, Berkeley, Calif. The Triplet Connection

can create a choking hazard, be sure to watch your babies when using any hands-free feeding system. Podee bottles can be found at Toys R Us.

DIAPERS AND MORE DIAPERS!

Oh yes, the diapers. Diapers for multiples are a *BIG* expense. You can never have too many, and your radar for diaper deals seems to intensify with each baby bottom you change.

DIAPER DRIVES

This is a fantastic way to help expectant parents stockpile a good supply. Brand and size don't matter, my friend. They will all be used eventually. Here are some examples of how a diaper drive works.

- Create a raffle system for each package of diapers donated.

- Have co-workers send a broadcast e-mail announcing a Diaper Donation Drive. Set up a large colorful open box in the cafeteria or break room.

- Make arrangements with your church to place a large diaper donation box in the church foyer.

"Tell the guests in advance and note on the baby shower invitations that for every package of diapers they bring, their name will be entered into a drawing. Make up some fancy gift baskets filled with baked goods and gourmet nuts, bubble baths and lotions, or fancy Italian pastas and gourmet olive oils. Use your imagination and raffle them off!"

—**KR, Wadsworth, Ohio**

"We were crossing the San Mateo Bridge in San Francisco and found ourselves in a major traffic jam. When we finally inched our way to the source, we discovered a truck that had lost part of its load. HUGGIES! Hundreds and hundreds of Huggies, scattered all across the San Mateo Bridge and into the bay! It was like green cash blowing in the wind!"

—**Sheila and Bill in Awe**

"I received boxes of diapers from people I didn't even know, but who knew of my pregnancy from family members or friends. Sometimes the UPS man would show up and deliver a small care package filled with diapers and supplies. Now, when I hear of a family expecting multiples, I give back by doing the same thing for a family I never have met."

—Sheila, Receiving and Giving

"Reserve a banquet room at a buffet-style restaurant and host a brunch baby shower. Add a great twist to the shower invitations by specifying on the invitations that the price of admission is one package of any size diapers."

—BS, Highland Heights, Ohio

PICTURES

Everyone wants a picture of the babies, and so do you! Great gift ideas include:

- Disposable cameras
- Lots of rolls of film
- A case of blank video tapes
- Gift certificates for photo processing from your local retailer
- Gift certificates for a sitting with a professional photographer
- Separate baby photo albums—one for each baby!
- Family photo albums for the whole gang!
- Picture frames—big and small
- Brag books
- A group gift of a 35mm camera or even a video camera!

PREPARED MEALS

When the babies arrive, you will be completely immersed, and there will be no time left for shopping and cooking. We can't emphasize enough what it means to have a meal just waiting to be heated up. The following contributors will attest to the fact that meals for the freezer make great shower gifts.

"I lost twenty pounds in the first three exhausting months between taking care of the babies and my wife during her recovery. Sleep was so precious, once the babies went down, I chose sleep over preparing a meal."

—Bill Sleep-eating

"Ask each guest to bring a frozen meal for the couple. You will have little time to prepare meals for yourself. A stocked freezer with ready-to-eat dinners will help you through a very emotionally and physically stressed time."

—DF, Long Island, N.Y.

"My sister-in-law set up a dinner shower. The people brought a dinner every other night for weeks. It was much more useful than designer outfits."

—JM, The Triplet Connection

"Ask whoever is organizing the meal program for you to ask the participants to deliver the meals in disposable containers. This small consideration means one less thing to deal with. You can throw them away and not worry about washing and returning the casserole dish or platter."

—MES, Moreland Hills, Ohio

CORDLESS TELEPHONE

If you don't have at least one of these, *make sure* it's on your baby shower wish list. For an extra special treat, get the hands-free cordless style.

THE GIFT OF TIME

Time will no longer be your own once the babies arrive. Gifts that save you time, or allow you to rest while someone else cares for the babies or cleans the house, are more valuable than anything else you will receive. Here are a few examples of "gifts of time" that will be appreciated.

> "The Ameritech tetherless, cordless phone with head-set is awesome! You can roam from room to room while talking on the phone and have <u>both</u> <u>hands free</u> to manage the babies. The headset and boom fits securely on your head. It's the best $200 I ever spent!"
> —KR, Wadsworth, Ohio

✖ A boilerplate word processing document requesting free stuff from all the manufacturers that offer multiple birth programs, along with pre-addressed and stamped envelopes. All Mom and Dad will have to do is enclose a copy of the birth certificates and send them.

✖ Baby shower thank you cards along with pre-addressed and stamped envelopes created from the list of baby shower attendees. Big time saver!

✖ An awesome gift idea is a private nurse for the first week at home.

> "My husband's parents paid for a night nurse for six weeks so we could get some sleep."
> —JB, Birmingham, Ala.

✖ A gift of any home cleaning service. Regardless of what kind of housekeeper you were before the babies arrived, housekeeping quickly gives way to the babies' simultaneous needs and demands. What were once daily household routines are neglected, and you find yourself living in a messier, more cluttered place than you were used to. A fresh once over through the house will be greatly appreciated.

- An occasional night of relief: A prepaid local hotel certificate along with an offer to spend all night caring for your babies is a gift that will be treasured.
- Ask Grandma or any other experienced relative to take one baby every now and then for the night. Taking only one baby off your hands is heavenly. It makes a huge difference in the demands on you.

"My sisters came to our house and pulled all-nighters while we checked into a hotel. We slept for fifteen hours."

—Sheila and Bill in a State of Exhaustion

"We checked into our hotel thinking we were going to have our first night alone together since the babies were born. At 8 o'clock we cracked open a bottle of wine. At 8:10 we were out cold."

—Confessions from Parents of Triplets

"The most valuable gift one can offer is time. After checking with the mom-to-be, if anyone wishes to give a gift of time, tell them to write something on the gift card such as, 'I'd like to give you three hours of nap time on Wednesday for two months.' Buying an item is nice, but it can't compare to someone giving you their time to make things more manageable or pleasant for a mother caring for three or more infants (or toddlers)."

—DF, Long Island, N.Y.

"On occasion, our sisters took one or all of the babies for the night at their homes, giving us a welcome night's relief. This far outweighed any amount of diapers, sleepers, or toys received."

—Sheila and Bill, Grateful

CLOTHES

Those tiny little outfits are so cute, but instead of newborn sizes, request larger sizes that they will grow into. The babies are likely to receive plenty of infant to six month hand-me-downs that are gently worn and in very good condition.

"By the time we got around to dressing them in anything other than sleepers, they had outgrown most of the adorable outfits we received. Many still had the tags on them."

—Triplet Mom, San Francisco, Calif.

A CONTRIBUTION TO THEIR COLLEGE FUND

Don't be shy about accepting money to help their future. Immediately put any gift money in a special account for them.

HIGH TICKET ITEMS

Expensive items such as strollers, gliding rocking chairs, high chairs, 35mm cameras, or video cameras make excellent group gifts.

"The Boss" LITE Cordless Sweeper by Eureka is another item that will be used every day.

"If the expecting couple does not have a video camera, it's a good idea to try to figure a way to give them one as a gift. We did not have one and we regret not biting the bullet and making the payments. Perhaps one or two sets of grandparents can chip in and purchase it. It will give so much more pleasure than clothing, cribs, car seats, etc. A video camera will give years of wonderful memories."

—DF, Long Island, N.Y.

"Eureka's The Boss is a great invention! Between the myriad of graham crackers and Cheerios, this lightweight, portable sweeper will become your best friend!"

—BM, Hacienda Heights, Calif.

"Have everyone chip in for a good triplet stroller and fill it with diapers."

—JB, University Heights, Ohio

"Did Someone Say the 'M' Word?"—Minivans

Making the transition from a sporty two-seater to a *mmm… mmm…* minivan represents just one of the many, many sacrifices you will make for your children.

> *"Suburban—it's the only way to go."*
>
> **—JB, Birmingham, Ala.**

TIP!

Trade in the family car for a minivan. Period.

- Popular vans among us veterans include: Dodge Grand Caravan, Grand Voyager, Windstar, and Safari.
- Some like a full-size van. Be aware that the full-size vans are gas hogs and may not fit inside your garage.
- Full-size vans such as a Ford Econoline with a custom high top or Chevy Suburbans are more popular with families with other children in addition to their multiples.

> *"I traded in my pickup truck for a blue minivan and a handful of pacifiers."*
>
> **—Bill and the Blue Minivan**

TIP!

WAIT! Before you buy or register for car seats, go to a retail store and measure the width of various car seats. Find a style that is narrow enough so that all three car seats can fit side by side on one rear bench seat of your minivan. Now you can remove the first bench seat, which will open up extra room in the vehicle providing a larger area for access and storage of items like strollers and diaper bags.

✖ Split seats are recommended so you can maneuver around inside and gain access easily to the rear of the van.

✖ The most important consideration is that the triplet stroller or any combination of strollers fit behind the last seat or in the space between the driver and the babies.

> *"I loved my Grand Voyager, and now my Town & Country. They have sliding doors on both sides and lots of room for that stroller!"*
>
> —JB, University Heights, Ohio

✖ A TV and VCR for the van can be pricey but you'll get your money's worth! It entertains on long distance rides, especially when they get older, and keeps down the fussing and the fights.

TIP!

Depending on the make and model of your minivan, you can even use the interior open space in your van to park your uncollapsed double or triplet stroller. In bad weather this is especially helpful in that you can load all the children into the stroller while still inside the van, thus providing shelter from the elements as long as possible.

> *"We love our Suburban. Lots of extra space in the rear for sporting equipment."*
>
> —BL, Chagrin Falls, Ohio

> *"The bigger the better! If you only have triplets, take out the middle seat and place all three babies in the back seat. This will give you more room to move around."*
>
> —KD, N. Olmstead, Ohio

> *"To get that triplet stroller behind the rear seat of the van, remove the rear stroller seat and fold down its handle. You DO NOT have to disassemble the whole stroller and its fifty-two thousand parts!"*
>
> —Bill Putting the Stroller in a Full Nelson

"Been There, Done That"— Support Groups for Multiples

There are several national support organizations dedicated to families of multiples. They provide excellent information and inspiration for parents before and after the birth of multiples. We recommend that you contact these organizations because they can provide information and support on many topics including preterm labor, coping strategies if your babies are in NICU, and just managing from day to day. Their web sites and quarterly newsletters are loaded with articles, letters, and wonderful personal stories from families of multiples that will make you laugh and cry.

They can be especially helpful in locating a regional or local support group in your own community. You will meet the most amazing people, build life-long friendships, and learn from each other.

Mothers of Supertwins (MOST) is an international non-profit organization that provides a support network of families who have or are expecting triplets, quadruplets, or more. Twenty packets of information are available, along with empathy and good humor during pregnancy, infancy, toddlerhood, and school age. MOST offers telephone support during pregnancy, issues a quarterly publication filled with articles, and provides information and research results from multiple birth families and professionals.

    P.O. Box 951
    Brentwood, NY 11717-0627
    (516) 859-1110
    www.mostonline.org

       NOMOTC—National Organization of Mothers of Twins Clubs, Inc. A network of over 400 clubs with nearly 20,000 members nationwide. Call for a free brochure listing local support groups in your community. Thirty-five years strong!

    P.O. Box 23188
    Albuquerque, NM 87192-1118
    (800) 243-2276
    www.nomotc.org

The Triplet Connection is a national support organization that provides valuable information to families who are expecting triplets or more. A *"Network of Caring and Sharing,"* The Triplet Connection provides resources, encouragement, and a supportive network for families of higher order multiples who are willing to share their experiences. The Triplet Connection manages the largest database of higher multiples in the world. They provide an *"Expectant Mother's Packet"* of information that contains helpful information regarding preterm birth prevention and pregnancy-related concerns, as well as information for new parents after the birth. Their quarterly newsletter is filled with articles and letters that any parent of multiples will appreciate and enjoy.

    P.O. Box 99571
    Stockton, CA 95209
    (209) 474-0885
    www.tripletconnection.org

Chapter Three

"Will They Ever Sleep Through the Night?"— The First Six Months

"Keeping the Faith"—Coping Strategies While They're in the NICU

Having your babies go into the neonatal intensive care unit (NICU) is a highly emotional experience, filled with worry, hope, and lots of prayers. All premature babies are different, but they can and do thrive; and we hope your children will come home with you promptly. Here, parents share some of their stressful moments and their coping strategies while their babies were in the NICU.

"While my babies were in the NICU, bringing in my breast milk at feeding times and bringing in musical toys and bright rattles helped me feel closer to them. Enjoy your sleep during this time!"

—JJ, Brandenton, Fla.
The Triplet Connection

"We filled their incubators with photos of me and my husband and with special toys for each of them, to make them feel that we were always with them."

—KD, N. Olmstead, Ohio

"Emotionally, it was extremely hard. I went to visit them as often as I could.... There were times (especially in the wee hours) when I couldn't stand to be away from them and I would drive to the hospital to sit with them for a few hours."

—DB, Puxico, Mo.

"I purchased a small cassette player and tiny speakers for each baby's bed unit and recorded various tapes (whale sounds, Kenny G., lullabies). I also got each of them a soft bunny, and they are still attached to them today. I purchased several disposable cameras to leave at the hospital for the nurses to take pictures in my absence."

—DB, Puxico, Mo.

"We Did It!"—Coming Home

The physically and emotionally exhausting experience of giving birth, compounded by being cooped up twenty-four hours a day, seven days a week and running on empty, can cause even the best prepared mothers to get into a real funk.

 **TIP!**

Going from *very pregnant* to *unpregnant* can be a major adjustment for the body and soul.

More than 50 percent of women experience postpartum blues, which is different than postpartum depression. On the third or fourth day after delivery, symptoms including tearfulness, tiredness, sadness, and difficulty thinking clearly can indicate the blues. It can last from several days to several weeks. Most of these symptoms are common reactions to the change in hormone levels after giving birth, dealing with the new babies, and operating on very little sleep, not to mention the stress of the delivery process itself. These baby blues usually clear in one to three weeks as hormone levels return to normal and the mother develops a routine and a sense of control.

For a small percentage of women, one to two percent, it lingers on and on. Postpartum depression is different from the baby blues. If you experience prolonged depression, and the symptoms don't resolve by the time the baby is one month old, don't hesitate to talk to your doctor; he or she can help. You're not alone.

Coming home with an armful of babies means planning ahead. If these are your first babies, the transition from couple to family can be frightening.

LET GO AND LET OTHERS

Call it character building, call it what you want, but caring for multiple babies is monumental and no one person can do it alone.

"Even with help, I cried every day."

—Sheila

- ❖ Let others help out in any way they can.
- ❖ Let them pull shifts for you.
- ❖ Seize the opportunity to sleep when they're there.
- ❖ Resist the temptation to socialize and marvel over the babies together. You'll need your energy later, in the middle of the night.
- ❖ Don't push yourself. A Cesarean is major surgery, and just when you think that you have recovered, you may to find yourself slammed back into bed.

Refuse No Offers! —Accepting and Organizing Volunteer Help

SAY "YES!" AND PLUG 'EM IN

❋ When the offers of help come in, seize the moment and accept them.

❋ Follow through by asking when, specifically, they can help. Drill right down to the day, the morning or after-noon, and what hours.

❋ Create a schedule—if possible, do this before birth. Schedule the offers to help as they come in. Three hours here, four hours there. Believe me, you will be so busy managing the babies that a simple tool such as a schedule can be a lifesaver. With the lack of sleep due to around the clock care and feeding, there will be many occasions when you literally will not know what day it is.

❋ If possible, distribute a "Help Wanted" list among family and friends before birth. Load it with suggestions including cooking, cleaning, baby shifts, shopping, and more.

❋ Although this may not always be possible, stagger your donated help, making it last as long as possible. Plug in the gaps with hired help. This will keep people from offering to help at the same time, so you won't be left for long stretches without an extra pair of hands.

❋ Remember, people want to help, and politely saying *"no, thank you"* because you are shy, or not accustomed to accepting so many offers, denies them of the pleasure of helping others.

TIP!

Your multiples will teach you many things, and one of their gifts is teaching you to be humble and let others do for you.

"I was such a zombie, sometimes people would show up at my door and I had no idea that they told me they were coming over to help that day."

—Sheila, Sleepwalking

"I kept a photocopied copy of a calendar on my kitchen cabinet by the phone. When people called and offered to help, I had it in front of me to sign them up."

—KD, N. Olmstead, Ohio

LINE UP THE A-TEAM

If you are lucky and have family members in the same town, you may have parents or siblings who are willing to stay with you for days and even weeks.

> **TIP!**
>
> **Sleep when you are off-duty. Let your housework go and sleep instead. Your house will look a lot better when you've had some sleep. Even if it is high noon, sleep for an hour or two and do nothing else.**

BE SPECIFIC

Divide up the shifts and assign specific duties to each member of the team, and keep a record of who's on duty for which feedings. Give your volunteers specific tasks:

- keeping up with the laundry
- making formula
- stocking diapers
- preparing meals
- charting the babies' consumption and output
- running errands

The A-Team will be overwhelmed too, and may not know how you want things done. As you learn along the way what routines and techniques work best for you and the babies, explain them to the helpers and they'll quickly get the hang of it.

LITTLE THINGS MEAN LOT

Friends who have no experience caring for babies, or grandparents who may be too old or unable to adapt to the chaos multiples bring, can still provide the much-needed help in other ways that do not involve directly caring for the babies. In your situation, little things mean a whole lot, and occasional help with errands, returning or exchanging duplicate gifts at the store, housekeeping, and cooking make a difference.

IF YOU'RE COMING OVER, EXPECT TO HELP!

Expect visitors, neighbors, baby-starved friends, and curiosity seekers to drop in, announced and unannounced.

> **TIP!**
>
> **Like a glass of water to a drowning man, the last thing you need to do at this time is socially entertain visitors and give lessons on how to hold and feed a baby. So put them to work!**

Here are a few suggestions for dealing with visitors:

- Ask people to call before they come by—so your cherished naps are not interrupted.
- Suggest they come at feeding time or bath time so they can participate.
- When they ask *"Is there anything I can do—do you need anything?"* say *YES!* Ask them to bring over a casserole, take-out food, groceries, or to pick up a six-pack of diapers!
- Ask them to take a baby for an outing during their awake time.
- Suggest that they care for your babies while you *sleeeep*.

"Be up front with friends and family about your expectations. If you don't, the next thing you know you will be asking if you can get them something to drink, offering them something to eat, and suddenly you're entertaining, adding more stress to the situation. Have them get in the trenches with you!"

—KR, Wadsworth, Ohio

"Remember, in the beginning there is no time for social visits. All visitors should expect to help."

—KD, N. Olmstead, Ohio

"We put Grandpa in charge of making formula. At the rate we went through formula, this became a very important job! It gave him a way to participate in a very helpful way. He always made sure there was fresh formula on hand and poured into bottles in time for the feedings. As time passed, even Gramps got comfortable with changing diapers!"

—MH, Lakewood, Ohio

KEEP GERMS OUT!

You are busy enough as it is! A merry-go-round of coughs, colds, flu, or other less pleasant ailments that could have been prevented by limiting unnecessary exposure is not what you need.

- ✖ Instruct people not to come by if they, a family member, or a co-worker has been ill in the last two weeks.

- ✖ Insist that people wash their hands before handling the babies. When one gets sick, they all get sick. Imagine, Baby One comes down ill with a three-day bug. Baby Two gets it two to three days later. Baby Three gets it soon thereafter.

TIP!

Like an Olympic baton that gets passed in the race, a three-day bug has now expanded into a week-long sickness extravaganza as it cycles through all of the children. Not to mention Mom and Dad!

- ✖ Post signs at the door and by the sink asking people to wash their hands.

"I would also recommend that you make a large sign that is visible as soon as you come in the door that states that everyone should wash their hands thoroughly prior to handling the babies. We kept anti-bacterial soap and paper towels by the sink to try to keep germs away. We found that people were very understanding about our request, and we did not have any problems."

"After the birth of our quadruplets, our pediatrician recommended that we try to limit their exposure to others until they reached ten pounds. Having the doctor say this made it easier to spread the word that 'Dr. H. said we should not have many visitors.'"

—Mother of Quadruplets
Decatur, Ala.

EVERYONE HAS THEIR OWN LIVES

A combination of friends and family will offer to help, but, realistically, they may not always be available. Understandably, they are consumed by their own families and their daily lives.

> "When the babies are born and come home you will be surrounded by family, friends, and many visitors. There is a lot of excitement and the telephone rings off the hook. But much like a funeral, after the event, people who offered their support start to fade away, and you are left to cope with the responsibility, alone, without any sleep."
>
> —KR, Wadsworth, Ohio

> "My first advice is not to count on the many friends who have offered to babysit. We found that all of those offers pretty much evaporated when the kids were actually born and came home. The ones you can really count on are your relatives and the paid help."
>
> —ST, Father of Triplets, Calif.

"Worth Their Weight In Gold"— Finding Quality Hired Help

FACE IT, YOU ARE OUTNUMBERED

Toss the myth of "self-sufficiency" and acknowledge your need for help.

If it takes one set of parents to raise one baby, then the following ratios should apply for multiples:

Twins	four adults!
Triplets	six adults!
Quads	eight adults!
Quints	ten adults!

So if you're going at this alone while your spouse is at work, you will need help!

GET AS MUCH HIRED HELP AS YOU CAN AFFORD!!

If there is one idea you take with you from this book, let it be this. The days of the extended family with the built-in babysitter are gone. If you have this arrangement, consider yourself lucky. Factors such as our mobile society and job transfers create geographical distances between families. The lack of access to a supportive family network is compounded by demanding careers and the need for dual incomes. Most parents of multiples find themselves on their own without any sleep.

"I remember not being able to give someone simple directions to my house due to lack of sleep and long-term fatigue. I was so fried, I could not explain how to make a 'right at the stop sign and then a quick left after the big red house on the corner.'"

—SL, Fairfield, Calif.

TIP!

Help is not a luxury, help is a necessity.

Yes, it is expensive, very expensive, but get as much help as you possibly can afford, especially during the first six months, even if it is just a few hours a day. Keep in mind that it is temporary. An extra pair of hands will make a tremendous difference. It can save your marriage and your sanity, and most important, it can enhance the quality of your children's lives. One thing is certain, keeping up with two, three, four, or more babies is a *HUGE* task; don't underestimate this. You will be so exhausted that simple things such as getting showered and dressed can become monumental.

Extra help will give you the much-needed break you need for sleep and to take care of yourself. It will be essential for your mental and physical health. It will help you be more patient with the babies and your partner.

Finding Hired Help

If you have not done this before the birth, blanket the community with news about the babies' birth and put out as many feelers in your community for help as possible.

Word of mouth is very powerful. Advertise in your local newspaper, notify your church, advertise at local high schools and colleges, and contact other parents of multiples in your community for referrals.

> "Most people do not understand what a wonderful but tiring job triplets are! Try to get as much help as you can in the beginning."
>
> —JJ, Brandenton, Fla.
> The Triplet Connection

Nannies

For the financially fortunate families that can afford one, a full-time nanny may offer the best solution. But nannies who are willing to take on multiples are few and far between, and *they will be expensive*. It takes a special nanny to handle the demands of multiple babies and to *stay cool* when they all get wound up at the same time!

There are many agencies listed in the Yellow Pages that, for a fee, will help you in your search. They will provide full background information including credit history, traffic violations, criminal history, and previous employment. Set the expectations up front by writing out a full job description.

> "The greatest help that I have had is a wonderful nanny. She came to work for us when the boys had been home about two weeks, and is still with us. I tell my husband she has more job security than he does!"
>
> —Mother of Quadruplets
> Decatur, Ala.

IN-HOME CARE

Our experience with child care is that there are more people who are willing to have you come to their home than are willing to come to yours. With so many infants, just getting them ready and out the door every morning can be difficult! Many families use part-time high school or college students, work around their schedules, and give them the hours they want. Some families have had great success with au pairs, while others describe the experience as being like "raising a teenager," and have the war stories to support it.

COMPANY ON-SITE CHILD CARE

They are few and far between. If we were running the company, we would make it happen. The employee loyalty alone would be worth it, from a business perspective! Many parents are even willing to take a pay cut to have on-site care. But most importantly, the quality of family life would be improved. If you have this benefit available to you, treasure it.

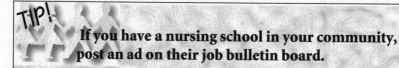

TIP!

If you have a nursing school in your community, post an ad on their job bulletin board.

HELP DURING "THE WITCHING HOUR"

If you can only afford a minimum amount of help, have them come in from 5:00 P.M. to 9:00 P.M. This seems to be the time when most parents are at the end of their rope, and is also the time when the babies tend to be the most fussy or when the wrath of colic arises. And if you can find a student who is willing to sit at night, from 8:00 P.M. to 2:00 A.M. for example, while you sleep, you have hit the lotto!

"We were extremely lucky to find three highly qualified, mature students in a graduate pediatric nursing program. This was a win-win combination in that they were highly qualified individuals, studying pediatrics, who were very knowledgeable and experienced in working with babies. At the same time, we provided flexible part-time work that appealed to their interests. We were able to schedule their help around their classes, vacations, and special interests—the key is to be flexible. We couldn't have done it without you, Kristin, Jen, and Jen!"

—Sheila and Bill

References and Preferences

Most parents tell us they have hired and fired many helpers. Bottom line: it is all in the qualification process up front and in the luck of the draw. Get at least three references and take the time to call them. Have a list of questions prepared in advance. Ask about their experience and education. Watch to see how they interact with your babies. Our best sitters have always immediately interacted with them. Take the time during the interview to learn their hobbies and interests, and, of course, do they smoke or drink? If their first question is *"How much do you pay?"* close the interview. You know the questions to ask, they're your babies!

Pay Them Well

Yes, the cost of help is high. Keep things in perspective, however, by realizing that it is short term. Go heavy on the help the first six

> *"I would set up an interview and if I liked them, I had a trial run with them. I had five separate people come in each day of the week to see how they were with my kids and to see if they made themselves at home. I found out that mothers were better than young women because they knew what it was like to have kids and run a household. Your nanny is going to become your friend and is going to become attached to your children. You want someone who is loving and affectionate and responsible."*
>
> **—GW, Fairfield, Calif.**

"Pay the sitter well—you've spent money on worse things."
—BT, N. Olmstead, Ohio

months, even if it is just a couple of hours a day. In the long term, it will pay off in better physical and emotional health for you and the babies. As time passes, you will become more experienced in managing the babies and their simultaneous demands. When this happens, you will be able to taper off the hired help.

TIP! If you feel you can't make it through the first six months, and you own your home, consider taking out an equity line of credit to support the cost of help. You will only need help for a short period of time. Then you will be able to begin paying back the loan.

HELP FROM THE KID NEXT DOOR

When your babies are older, find a neighborhood family with a ten- to twelve-year-old. Arrange to have him or her come over and play with your toddlers under your supervision. This keeps the babies occupied while you can look after a few other things. This is a win-win arrangement for everyone involved. It's great fun for all the kids and gives the parents of both families a little breathing room.

> "We've also had a schoolgirl here for a few hours so I can do laundry or cook dinner. Try to schedule her during their play time so if she is twelve to fifteen years old you will feel comfortable."
>
> —KD, N. Olmstead, Ohio

"Navigating the Zombie Zone"— Surviving Sleepless Nights

Stop and think about it. Each baby needs to be fed seven to eight times a day—each baby!!! Each baby needs to be changed eight to ten times a day. Each baby needs to be loved... and so on and so on.

TIP!

Multiply all this by two, three, four, or more and suddenly you find yourself up twenty-four hours a day, seven days a week, running on empty, with no days off, vacation, or sick time.

Our three babies were on a three-hour schedule, and with lots of practice, we got our feeding times down to a record forty-five minutes to one hour. This left one and a half, or, at best, two hours to sleep, only to be awakened to start the cycle all over again. Add a little gas and colic, and you're on the verge of a serious tailspin!

Most parents tell us that the chronic sleep deprivation during the first six months is the most difficult aspect of caring for multiples. Until your babies start sleeping through the night, the lack of sleep is *brutal*. Unless you have the

> "The marathon of broken sleep was worse than the lack of sleep."
>
> —MR, Canton, Ohio

luxury of round-the-clock, full-time help, you will go through this time as a complete delirious zombie. Welcome to the club.

We quickly looked for ways to be as efficient as possible in the middle of the night, when the chronic fatigue was at its peak, so that we could *squeeze* in as much extra sleep as possible.

> "I missed the whole winter that year. At three or four o'clock in the morning I would look outside the nursery window as I fed my babies and watch the snow come down. Our house was the only house in the neighborhood with a light on."
>
> —Sheila, In the Still of the Night

> "I remember many times when I had to look at a newspaper or catch a glimpse of the news on TV to know what day is was."
>
> —Bill in a Blur

TAKE SHIFTS

Be on "Baby Patrol" from 10:00 P.M. to 2:00 A.M. While you manage the nursery, the feedings, the diapering, and the formula preparation, your partner sleeps. Switch every four to six hours.

> "My husband and I took turns getting up with all three so one of us could sleep."
>
> —SN, New Philadelphia, Ohio

> "To all those expectant moms out there or those with babies under six months, hang in there! It gets a lot easier. Spoken by an ex-zombie with experience in sleep-feeding, sleep-changing, and sleepwalking."
>
> —CC, Orange, Calif.
> The Triplet Connection

"We became like two ships passing in the night. Whoever was on baby watch would wake the other from their deep sleep and change shifts. The exhausted one would plop into bed for their coveted interval of rest. Very few words were ever spoken, only the usual, 'Honey, it's your turn.'"

— Sheila and Bill, The First Six Months

More Middle of the Night Tips!

- Save as much energy as possible for tomorrow.
- Keep the lighting dim. Use the stove light; or use an aquarium as a night-light and a source of soothing sound.
- You'll undoubtedly find many more tricks and techniques to help you make it through those overwhelming months of non-stop demands. Parents of multiples are, by necessity, innovative.

"We purchased a small dormitory/apartment refrigerator and put it in the boys' room for their bottles. We used an electric bottle warmer to warm them. It kept us from having to run downstairs in the night."

—BT, Belleville, Ill.
The Triplet Connection

"Feed now, wash later. Put the empties in the dishwasher to be dealt with tomorrow, just like you did in the olden days when you'd put off cleaning up after the party until the next morning."

—Triplet Mom,
San Francisco, Calif.

"We made up a twenty-four hour supply of formula every day, in color-coded bottles, and packed a small ice chest with reusable blue ice to take upstairs at night. We warmed the bottles in the bathroom sink filled with hot water, and often fed the babies in our bed."

—CB, Linden, Calif.
The Triplet Connection

"We'll try anything once. If it's a disaster, we'll try it again next week or next month. We never push our babies, but they grow and change so quickly that what doesn't work at eight weeks may work beautifully at twelve weeks."

—KR, Wadsworth, Ohio

"To save time in the middle of the night, prop the bottles and feed all three at the same time. I never leave them unattended and I have two hands to adjust, help, or burp whoever is ready. Have bottles pre-made and have everything ready for the feeding before you go to bed. Leave the lights off, use only a hall light, don't talk to the children, put a larger size diaper on the babies when they go to bed, and do not change them in the middle of the night (unless it is absolutely necessary)."

—NJ, Macedonia, Ohio

SLEEPING ARRANGEMENTS

The babies have been together from the very beginning, long before even you knew they were nestled together in the womb. There is a special bond between them that will remain throughout life. Multiples who have lost one of their own report that they still feel the connection and know what the one who has departed off to heaven would have done and said had he or she been here physically on earth.

They've been with each other since the beginning of it all, why separate them now?

- Start out in the same crib, lay them crosswise with wedgies or rolled up receiving blankets between them. They seem to like the snug fit and their cries do not disturb each other.
- There will come a time, when they are around three or four months old, that they will become too long to lay crosswise in the crib and you will need to move each baby into his or her own crib.
- Even if you have a *HUGE* house with separate bedrooms for each man, woman, and child of the family, they can share a bedroom for a long time to come. They love it, because they can have a party babbling back and forth over their crib rails like neighbors across the backyard fence.

"I keep telling myself that I'm going to put the video camera in the nursery so I can get on film exactly what is so funny when they wake up from their naps. When I open the nursery door you can hear a pin drop and they all look at me with blank expressions, as if they are all saying, 'What?'"

—Sheila Peeking in

"Long rectangular laundry baskets are a great inexpensive substitute for bassinets. We cut foam padding to fit the bottom of each basket and covered it with a pillowcase. When they outgrow the baskets you can use them for laundry, toy storage, and even playtime, as the babies love to fill them with items and push them back and forth across the floor."

—MH, Lakewood, Ohio

"Since we have a two-story house, we decided to have the triplets sleep downstairs during the day. For the first four to five months, the babies had their own sleeping area during the day—a bassinet, a cradle, and an old-fashioned buggy. Once the babies began rolling over and were more mobile, we purchased a four-by-six foot piece of two-inch-thick foam. The 'daybed' is surrounded by a portable play-yard called a 'Crawlspace.'"

—BC, Shippensburg, Penn.
The Triplet Connection

"I've Only Got Two Hands!"— Keeping Up with Multiple Babies

The vision of a new parent peacefully cuddling and snuggling baby for hours at a time is never quite achieved when the parent is trying to manage several babies simultaneously. Keeping up with them is like living in a storm. It's comparable to a hurricane, as there are moments of peace and quiet like the eye of the hurricane. This time is often spent doing damage control and preparing for the next round of "baby storm." But hurricanes have seasons— the endless needs of your babies don't. You quickly start finding ways to cut corners and make calculated compromises in search of relief, while still making it work.

SCHEDULES, SCHEDULES, SCHEDULES

The number one priority is establishing a routine schedule for the babies. Get them on a schedule as soon as possible. Everything else revolves around this. The babies will learn what to expect each day, and it will give you a sense of order in what can otherwise be total chaos. Depending on your children's health, ask that the hospital nursery staff keep your babies on the same schedule, and continue it at home.

 TIP!   **Consistent routines mean more free time for you.**

> "Once they were on schedules, life overall was much simpler.... I had time to do other necessary things since I was not constantly feeding and/or dealing with sleep problems twenty-four hours a day, which can happen if they are not on a schedule."
>
> —DB, Puxico, Mo.

"As each baby comes home, get him or her on a schedule. If one woke early, I would try to get him to go back to sleep; but if not, everyone else had to get up. No matter what, stick to your schedule! If they are on your schedule you'll have more free time!"

—KD, N. Olmstead, Ohio

"A schedule was very hard for us at the beginning, but I don't know what we would do without it now. You kind of feel like you're torturing your children at first, but... the children adjust well and life gets better for the whole household."

—NJ, Macedonia, Ohio

CHANGE FIRST, FEED SECOND

Changing your babies before you feed them will minimize the perpetual confusion of "who's been changed and fed? First? Last? Not at all?" Or sometimes twice. When they're infants you will go through twenty-five to thirty diapers a day and it is very easy to loose track. Be consistent with this method.

CHART EVERYTHING

Chart feeding times, amounts consumed, bowel movements, sleeping increments. This will help you stay on a steady schedule, and it will show their progress as their tiny stomachs begin to take more food and slowly extend the time between feedings. It will also be helpful information when you visit your pediatrician.

"Make a log sheet. I kept mine in a three-ring binder with a tab for each baby with feeding times, how much formula they took, temperatures, medicines administered, diaper changes (it's hard to remember who just pooped!) It became our Bible!"

—KD, N. Olmstead, Ohio

Methods of Feeding

BREASTFEEDING

Breastfeeding two, three, or more babies can present funny little tactical challenges. There are several scenarios, and as each baby is different, you will have to decide what works best for you and your babies. We suggest you use the information available from the national support groups on breastfeeding multiples and decide for yourself. Many women successfully breastfeed all of their babies. MOST (Mothers of Supertwins) reports that "Fifty percent of supertwin mothers choose to breastfeed their babies, and do so for an average of two to three months"; ninety-four percent of MOST's membership are parents of triplets!

> "Don't let anyone talk you out of nursing, or say it can't be done. Not only is it possible to nurse three babies, it's wonderful. My advice, use a breast pump after the initial feeding so you can always have a bottle of breast milk available. Offer an occasional bottle but make nursing the primary method of feeding. Rotate the babies at each feeding so they each have a chance to be first at some point during the day. Keep a chart, indicating which side the baby nursed from, for how long, and in what order."
>
> —BL, Chagrin Falls, Ohio

BOTTLE FEEDING

Ah, yes, another art that must be learned. Bottle feeding several babies who can't hold their own bottles takes a delicate balance of basic gravity and pure will. To keep it from developing into a three-ring circus, here are some great tips:

Until the babies are old enough for high chairs, place the babies in their infant carriers at feeding time. Prop their bottles by molding receiving blankets around the bottles for support during feeding time.

Important Note: Never leave your babies unsupervised or unattended. If your babies have any preemie issues such as difficulty sucking or feeding, do not use any bottle-propping system.

The babies should never be fed lying on their backs and should never be put to bed with a bottle, as this can contribute to tooth decay and ear infections.

Before your babes can hold their own bottles, the Podee Hands-Free Baby Bottle will give you some freedom to do things like answer the phone or go to the bathroom. It may take a few tries to get them used to it, but after that you won't have to prop another bottle.

Eventually, the babies will start holding their own bottles and life gets a little easier, for now, but spoon feeding has its own challenges.

"An easy way to feed the babies when there is no one to help—set the infant car seats at the end of each crib, propping bottles, and go from one end to the other burping. When they are finished, leave them sitting upright for fifteen to twenty minutes for their tummies to settle. They then fall asleep, and I don't have to walk far to lay them down. The infant car seats fit nicely under the cribs."

—CF, Omaha, Neb.
The Triplet Connection

"We would 'jump start' the suction ourselves and then pass the nipple to the baby. They are great. We began using them at two weeks old."

—Sheila

"I thought I had reached Nirvana when they started to sit up and hold their own bottles."

—Kyle and Crew, Ariz.

BABY FOOD AND TABLE FOOD TRANSITIONS

Between four and six months, you can start introducing baby foods and by six to nine months you can begin table foods. When they reach this new stage, all the spit ups, formula stains, and every imaginable bodily fluid your little darlings could muster up when they were on bottles will be minuscule compared to what your highly opinionated little Rembrandts have in store for you as they experience new tastes and textures.

TIP!

Don't wear your Sunday best when feeding!

Like all babies, they will be more interested in playing with and feeling their food than eating it. With your crew of feeding babies, there will be enough flying sweet potatoes and peas, applesauce smears on the floor, and spaghetti spatters in their hair to qualify for a first-class paper towel TV commercial.

"You will have an infinite supply of those little jars that your dad used to use to neatly store little nuts and bolts in the garage. Don't be surprised when your wife asks you to deplete your supply by 50 percent when they fall out from underneath her side of the bed."

—KT, Chandler, Ariz.
The Triplet Connection

"I had to separate the babies by forming a circle with their high chairs so that they all faced each other. This way they could no longer grab each other's food or smear their own food into the other guy's hair."

—Bill in the Ring

"One jar, one bowl, one spoon. I tried separate jars, separate spoons, and separate bowls at first, but I gave up. Not enough hands."

—Sheila Surrenders

"One trick to help feed picky eaters is to distract them with something while you spoon feed their food into their mouths. We used small pieces of bread that they could pick up, squish, and play with. We also gave them a few lids to the baby food jars. The babies loved to clang them together and they were a very effective distraction."

—Bill

"When solids began, we tried one feeding dish divided into separate sections. Each section had their first initial, so we could keep track of who ate what."

—KM, Los Angeles, Calif.

SIPPY CUP TRANSITION

Sooner or later you will abandon the bottles and advance to training cups. Yes, bottles are easy, the babies love them, and besides, when they're fussing, pop a bottle in their mouths and everyone is happy, right? Short-term, yes, long-term, no.

Assuming your babies were not premature, somewhere around six months you can begin introducing the sippy cup. That doesn't necessarily mean they'll take it but it's a start. Holding multiple cups for multiple babies is another art you will soon master. Trying to hold onto two, three, or more baby's cups for them while they are seated in their high chairs eating finger food is another clip to consider for *America's Funniest Home Videos*.

❌ Always offer a cup feeding before a bottle feeding.

❌ Make the weaning process gradual, and set a goal to eliminate one bottle feeding per baby every three to four days.

- ❧ Eliminate bottle feedings in the following order to ease the adjustment: midday, late afternoon, morning, and finally bedtime.

- ❧ After eliminating the bottles, respond to their requests for a bottle by holding your babies or allowing a favorite toy.

"Success Formulas"—
Saving Time on Mixing and Heating

When they're finally all sleeping, you can sit down and relax, right? Well, not exactly. Not until you set up for the next round of feeding, and that means formula and bottle preparation.

> *"After all, you never really liked that silly game [of golf], and now you have bigger putts to sink. So, readjust your mindset and change your title from CEO of home entertainment to chief bottle washer and other duties as assigned. Yup, we veterans can boast of washing more Evenflos than a ninety-year-old bartender has soaked beer mugs."*
>
> **—KT, Gilbert, Ariz.**
> **The Triplet Connection**

SAVE TIME—MIX IT IN BATCHES!

Follow these steps once and mixing formula will be as easy as throwing a switch!

1. Count the number of scoops per large can of powdered formula. Determine the amount of water needed to mix the entire can by multiplying the number of scoops by the number of ounces of water per scoop as stated on the can.

2. Get a gallon size plastic jug, and purchase an oversized plastic funnel at an auto parts store.

3. Using the funnel, pour the pre-measured amount of water into the jug.

4. Take a waterproof marker and clearly mark the water line on the outside of the jug.

5. Using the funnel, pour the entire can of powdered formula into the jug and shake well.

The next time you make up a batch of formula, just fill the jug to the water line mark, pour in the whole can of powdered formula, and shake well!

> *"We found it very useful to make enough bottles up for two days at a time. Of course, depending on whether the babies ate six or seven times a day, that was thirty-six to forty-two bottles! On the alternate nights (when we weren't making bottles) we would give the babies a bath."*
>
> **—C and FC, Solon, Ohio**

SAVE TIME HEATING FORMULA!

Anyone who says, "Don't use a microwave to heat formula," has probably never raised a small troop of babies at the same time. Yes, it's true, microwaves can create hot spots in the liquid it is heating, but a few good stirs and gentle shakes will blend the formula evenly, and, of course, always check the temperature first before feeding it to the babies.

> *"Whoever said, 'Don't use a microwave to heat formula,' must still have a rotary phone!"*
>
> **—Sheila**

> *"You'll easily wear out the best microwave in the land and you will eventually mix the equivalent of an Olympic-size swimming pool of 'moo juice' for your tribe."*
>
> **—KT, Gilbert, Ariz.**
> **The Triplet Connection**

> **TIP!**
>
> **If you have an "Instant Hot" faucet feature built into your kitchen sink you can save a huge amount of time heating formula day or night. If you don't have an "Instant Hot" faucet, consider buying one. They're easy to install. Hey, listen! You guys are raising multiples, so everything else is easy.**

Here's how you're family will benefit from an "Instant Hot" faucet:

> *"A crock pot filled with warm water set on low is a great way to warm bottles."*
>
> —C and FC, Solon, Ohio

1. Mix a full can of the powdered formula in advance, but make it double concentrated by cutting the amount of water required in half.

2. Fill twelve, fifteen, eighteen... bottles halfway with the concentrated formula and keep them stored in the refrigerator.

3. In the middle of the night when you hear the cries of your babies and pull yourself out of your much needed deep sleep, remove the bottles of concentrate and add equal amounts of "Instant Hot" water and give the bottle a good shake. The hot water and the cold formula combined will give you the perfect warm bottle that your babies will love. Just make sure you test the temperature first.

> *"We also found it easier to use all the same kinds of bottles. It makes assembling caps and rings much easier! We washed all of our bottle caps, rings, and nipples in the dishwasher which was a real time-saver."*
>
> —C and FC, Solon, Ohio

> *"Try to find a formula all the babies can use. If you change formulas for one, try to change it for all. 'All for one, one for all.' Keeping different formulas straight on two hours of sleep is harder than you can imagine."*
>
> —Bill and the Winning Formula

"Switch formulas. Talk with your doctor about switching to a pre-digested formula. It's expensive and smells like yesterday's garbage, but it's a small price to pay for the added peace it may bring."

—Bill

"WARNING!! Be careful to put milk—NOT FORMULA—into your coffee. A mixed gallon of formula can look a lot like a gallon of milk in the middle of the night."

—It Happened to Me, Bill

Doctor's Visits—Make the Best of It

Doctor's visits with several babies can be very stressful at any age. An appointment for one baby can take a long time, but when you add a few more babies into the mix it can seem like a half day is spent at the doctor's office.

The babies must be examined individually, and managing the others while waiting their turn to be seen is a handful. The scene can become very chaotic. The best solution? Take them to the doctor one at a time. But let's get real... who has the time?? Here are some excellent tips for making the best of those trips to the doctor:

- Bring both of your parents, or any combination of family, friends, or sitters. It's best to have one adult per child. The office people often offer to hold a baby, but you cannot count on them to be available.

- Make the appointments at the babies' best time during the day. Perhaps after their mid-morning nap so that they're refreshed and can roll right into lunch after the doctor's visit.

TIP!

Avoid making the babies' appointments late in the day when the doctor is more likely to be behind schedule. If it works with your babies' schedules, try scheduling their appointment first thing in the morning before the doctor gets backed up.

- Bring their favorite toys to keep them occupied during the wait.
- Bring the triplet stroller or one single and one double. Even though it is difficult to maneuver inside the examination room, it gives them a contained place to sit while their brother or sister is being seen.
- If your children are afraid of the doctor, ask the doctor to remove his lab coat and relate to the child favorably.
- Buy a toy doctor's kit and let your children give their stuffed animals a check-up—this will help ease the fear.

"Screaming Sabrina"— Coping with Multiple Colic and Crying

Nothing can be more agonizing for a parent than an unstoppable screaming baby who doesn't respond to any of your efforts to soothe and calm. With two or more at the same time, the situation can get pretty hairy, especially if you are alone. Bouts of unexplainable crying that last one to two hours and occur up to twice a day in an otherwise healthy baby (not hungry, not sick, not in pain, etc.) is known as colic. No one really knows what causes colic in babies. It affects

"When people came over to our house to help, they would always ask, 'What's the first thing you do when you hear a baby cry?' The answer: Pee! Who knows when you're going to get another chance!"

—LL, Morrow, Ohio

about ten percent of babies in the first few months of life and generally lasts until the baby reaches three to five months old.

Many things can cause a baby to cry non-stop. The crying does not necessarily mean that the infant is suffering from colic. See a doctor immediately to determine the cause before trying anything on your own. A doctor may suggest a number of different things to treat colic, even changing your diet if you are breastfeeding. So the best thing is to start with a doctor's visit.

"One had colic; we took turns leaving the room for some peace and quiet."
—TG, Mentor, Ohio

"Mostly… I just tried to hold onto my own sanity until we got past that stage, as it DOES pass. Of course, then you are faced with new problems, challenges, etc. but that's the whole idea of being a parent, right?"
—DB, Puxico, Mo.

"I blocked her out… didn't bother me after I learned not to 'hear it.'"
—BT, N. Olmstead, Ohio

"A piece of advice a NICU nurse gave me, as she put it, 'a baby won't die from crying.' When they are all screaming and you feel like you are two seconds away from the psych ward, just walk away, go outside, get away from it, even if it is only for a few minutes. There were quite a few moments I truly thought I was going to lose it, and I took her advice; I just walked outside and stood there for a few moments—it gave me a chance to catch my breath—and guess what, all three kids survived it!"
—DB, Puxico, Mo.

MAKE IT STOP!

Hang in there. Some parents tell us that they can mentally compartmentalize the stress and "turn it off" in their minds. My threshold for multiple simultaneous crying was not as high as Bill's and I prayed for patience and endurance. Our little girl, Sabrina, had colic symptoms as an infant, and she cried constantly, sometimes for hours. We had to walk and walk and walk her with her tummy cradled across Bill's arm to get her to sleep. Sometimes is seemed that she finally fell asleep from pure exhaustion.

EARPLUGS

Get yourself several sets of earplugs. Keep them in a place where you can find them quickly. Keep several sets in the minivan. With multiple wailing babies you're going to need them! Earplugs will give you the extra mile of patience when you need it.

"I found a style of earplugs that draped around my neck like a pair of sunglasses, when they weren't lodged in my head. When they turned up the volume, back in my ears they went."

—Bill on Mute

REDUCE THE STRESS IN THE BABIES' LIVES

Keeping the babies up and active with the hope that they will be worn out and fall fast asleep is likely to backfire. Over-stimulation and fatigue will soon fester into a stress reaction and it will be LOUD and CLEAR when they "hit the wall." They will not be able to calm themselves down and their stress will build.

"Every baby's tolerance to stimulation and activity is different. With multiples, you can't assume that the threshold of stimulation for one will apply to the others. Be aware of the amount of activity and stimulation the babies are getting, and watch for any indication that a baby is reaching his or her limits. When you start to see it coming, nip it in the bud and calmly soothe them and lay them down for a rest."

—KR, Wadsworth, Ohio

WHITE NOISE, VIBRATIONS, AND MOVEMENTS

Babies will sometimes respond to the craziest things. Just as some people do aerobics to reduce stress while others relax with a good book, babies respond to various stress-relieving tactics differently depending on their personalities.

Try all of these. Switch, alternate, and try various combinations, but never leave the babies unattended.

> "When all else fails, cry along with them."
> —Sheila

❉ Turn on the TV and tune into a static "snow" channel.

❉ Turn on the microwave and pop some popcorn and watch the "snow" together.

❉ Tune the radio in between stations and make it a real blizzard.

❉ Run the vacuum cleaner—you may need to run it for a while, so you might as well get out the attachments and get busy.

❉ Turn on the exhaust fan.

❉ Turn on the dryer, place the babies in their infant carriers or bouncy seats on top of it and let it "hum."

❉ Run the tap water in the sink, tub, or shower until the cows come home.

❉ Take a car ride and don't forget your earplugs.

❉ Load them up and go for a walk outside in the stroller (and let the neighbors watch!) Sometimes they respond to the change in environment and fresh air. Plus, the crying seems less loud outdoors!

❉ If it's just one, do laps together around the dining room and kitchen in the umbrella stroller.

❉ Swings! Crank 'em up and let 'em rock.

❉ Vibrating bouncy seats—at least you don't have to put in a quarter.

❉ Place the baby face down, resting on a warm water bottle against your forearm, and rock.

❉ Different rocking motions can produce different effects.

✖ Rock and walk, rock and walk, earplugs in, rock and walk.

✖ Use a calm gentle voice and talk softly to them. *"Mommy's here... Daddy's here...."*

✖ Give them a blanket to snuggle or a bottle.

TIP!

Never be afraid to call. Any questions or concerns whatsoever about the babies' health, development, nutrition, etc., should always be directed to their primary care pediatrician or nurse practitioner.

SLEEP TRAINING

Rocking the babies to sleep can be a calming experience, but it usually turns into a bad habit, as the babies are likely to become dependent on you in order to fall asleep. Unless this is how you want to spend every night, it's a good idea to teach your babies how to fall asleep on their own. Unless the babies were premature, by four to five months they no longer require nighttime feedings, making this a good time to start making the transition to sleeping through the night. Here are some helpful tips:

✖ As each baby starts to drift off, try gently lowering them into their cribs in a dark quiet room with a night-light. When they start to make a fuss, resist the temptation to pick up the babies. Instead try stroking them or whispering softly.

✖ Middle of the night contacts should be brief and boring; go in only if the baby cries for more than five minutes, but don't take him or her out of the crib or start playing. A few soothing words or a gentle back rub—no longer than a minute—should soothe the transition.

✖ Tiptoe out.

✖ As long as they are fed, safe, dry, and not sick, it is OK to let the babies cry. With the night-light, you can check on them every five to ten minutes without disturbing them.

- Follow your instincts if you think one of the babies is clearly upset. Remember, every baby is different and each will adjust to this new routine at their own pace.
- As they become used to this routine, you will be able to spend less time rocking and soon you will be able to just put the babies down for the night. They will learn that it is bedtime and not playtime. Each baby is different and some will respond quickly, in a matter of days, and for others it may take several weeks. If you stick it out and don't deviate or give in, they will start sleeping through the night. This also helps the babies put themselves back to sleep when they wake up in the night as all babies do. The key is to stick with the program.
- Enjoy your extra time to yourself.

Long-Term Advice

Upon the arrival of the babies into your life, the noise level in your household has been permanently turned up. Today it may be the crying, another year from now it will change to screaming and fighting, and someday it will be the stereo.

TIP!

The best tactic is to raise your threshold for noise, get into the zone, put yourself on "ignore," and get on with your day.

"Just think, you don't need to go to the ball park now to hear the roar of the crowd. No more parking hassles and rude fans port to stern. Now you have pure unadulterated volume cracking through your household like a Japanese bullet train."

—KT, Gilbert, Ariz.
The Triplet Connection

"Learn to ignore it. It just turns into multiple talking and fighting later on."

—JB, University Heights, Ohio

"Welcome to HELL Week"— Pulling the Binky Plug

PACIFIERS—A CONTRADICTION IN TERMS

> "Never insert into the mouth of a contented baby…. I weaned them off by five months—just because I couldn't find them."
> —GW, Fairfield, Calif.

They are one of the best and worst inventions. Babies have an instinct known as the sucking reflex for the around the first four months of their lives. There comes a time when they no longer have the need to suck, but simply enjoy the pacifying comfort it brings. A good rule of thumb is to begin decreasing the pacifier use around the time the babies are starting to crawl at about six to eight months, at which time it is recommended to use them only for naps or during sleep.

RESIST THE TEMPTATION!

When the babies fuss, it's easy to reach for the "plugs of silence." If you give into this after six to eight months, then the dependency begins. Multiple babies mean multiple binkies. Multiple binkies mean *Perpetual Pacifier Patrol,* as you spend most of your time policing that piece of plastic that is now ruling your life!

TIP!

You will now be a slave to the pacifier, and you will find yourself—dressed in silk suits or clean white pressed dress shirts—on your hands and knees reaching behind sofas and minivan seats in search of the almighty binky.

> *"Never put them to bed with one. If they get used to the pacifier, then they will wake you in the middle of the night just to find the pacifier."*
>
> —GW, Fairfield, Calif.

SLEEP TRAINING AND WITHHOLDING THE BINKY

Now what do you do when several babies randomly pop the binky out of their mouths (or worse, lose them) and fuss and cry until you find it ? It's the middle of the night, after a 2:00 A.M. feeding, you plug the babies, and you and the little darlings all drift off to sleep, right? Oops! Pacifier number one pops out— *Wha!!* You pull your exhausted body out of bed, replug, and return to your warm bed. You start to drift off and oops! this time pacifier number two slips out and once again you are up. This goes on and on, you're up and you're down, you're up and you're down, and soon it is time for the next feeding and guess who hasn't had any sleep?

TIP!

Bill chose to lose the plugs and teach the children to fall asleep on their own at the same time. He called it *"HELL WEEK."*

First, he waited until Mom was out of town so he would have only three babies to deal with. Then, he "lost" all the binkies (in a dresser drawer). With his trusty earplugs at his side he prepared for the showdown. When bedtime came and everyone was fed and changed, he did it. He laid them down talking softly to them the whole time—cold turkey—no twenty-six-mile stroll and no binky. He left the room, put in his magnum earplugs, and stayed close outside the bedroom door. Although he could still hear the crying, he was determined to endure it for ten straight minutes or die trying. He did it. Then he went in and, to his surprise, he was able to calm them down without picking them up. Quietly leaving again, it wasn't long until they regrouped and attacked his ear-drums again. He repeated the cycle a few times and then they were asleep. Then the surprise attack! In the middle of the night they awoke. NO BINKIES!!! Bill waited a few minutes and crept in soothing them with just a calm voice and a gentle touch (earplugs firmly lodged in his ears). This cycle repeated for three days and then it was over. When Mom came home and bedtime approached, all three went down without a fuss and slept though the night.

LOSE 'EM!

If you're not as brave as Bill, wean them off the pacifiers before the babies are nine months old. Offer them only at naptime or at night but get them off the binky around nine months and the babies won't remember the pacifier later on.

TIP!

Important Note: Never alter the pacifier in such a way that could any piece of it could be sucked off and choked on.

"When you know the only reason that they are crying is because of the missing pacifier, let them cry. Pat them on the back, hold them, but don't give in. The binky is you. We followed this approach at six months and within two to three days it was as if they never existed."

—GW, Fairfield, Calif.

"Alter the pacifier in some way, such as cutting the top or base of the tip. This will not offer the same sucking satis-faction, making it easier to take away and less rewarding to give back."

—Binky Bill

CHILDREN ARE GREAT NEGOTIATORS

For sanity's sake, some parents choose to allow the "plugs of silence" until the children get older. But then you will be faced with the challenging task of negotiating with each child and believe it, as they get older, this task gets harder.

> "To 'kick the habit' we talked about it regularly with the kids for a couple months and would offer them the chance to go without them. They finally agreed at naptime and though they tried to back out of it, we held them to what they had said. This went on and off for about a week, until naptime was without them. We then finally got an agreement for bedtime, and again, had to hold them to it. We had one very bad night with a lot of crying and little sleep, the second night was much better... but by the third night, plugs were history."
>
> —DB, Puxico, Mo.

"Out of sight, out of mind. Now I only use them at sleep time. Hey! I get eight hours of sleep if I use them!"
— KD, N. Olmstead, Ohio

"Two of mine still have binkies (twenty-one months)—If it makes them happy, let them have them!"
—TG, Mentor, Ohio

"They were three when they gave them up. We had a ceremony and said good-bye."
—JB, Birmingham, Ala.

"We told them to 'stay in your bedroom if you want it in your mouth.'"
—BT, N. Olmstead, Ohio

Chapter Four.

"Life Will Never Be the Same!"— Your New Lifestyle

"Facing Reality"—Adjusting to a Massive Lifestyle Change and House Arrest

Life will now be measured in inches, ounces, number of diaper changes, noses wiped, loads of laundry done, and hours slept. You will make countless compromises and sacrifices and you and your partner will negotiate over things you never *dreamed of.* Your friends will think you have disappeared from the face of the planet. At some level you will.

The babies' needs come first, and if there is a sliver of time left over, your needs come next. What were once your normal adult routines now get done occasionally, and sometimes not at all.

We had to relearn a few things, change our expectations of what can really get done, and work SLOWLY toward our personal plans and goals. We also learned some things along the way to minimize the hectic pace.

"I called my brother in Chicago to wish him a happy birthday and give him a friendly hard time about how he was pushing the 'Big Five-O.' He said, 'you're not exactly a spring chicken, you know, you're forty-one.' 'I am?' I said. I realized I had lost a whole year."

—Confession from a Father of Triplets

"You had better brace yourself. Remember the days when you used to slump in the easy chair, kind of rehashing your day with the remote control in your hand while your lovely wife made the evening meal? Well, I'm a nine-month veteran of the family influx game, and I'm here to tell you, you are going to be busy!"

—KT, Gilbert, Ariz.
The Triplet Connection

Keep Your To-Do List Short

With all the demands from the babies, the days of ticking off items on your list of "to-do's" are over. It's just not possible. For all the "Great Taskmasters" out there, this adjustment may be a rough one. Lower your expectations and keep your to-do list short.

"Sometimes it would be several hours after my shower before I even got around to combing out my hair."

—Sheila

Pick Only One At First

If there are four things on your to-do list and three or four errands or destinations on your partner's list, pick only one, and take turns. The good old days of "instant gratification" as you once knew it are gone—kaput! Even if you muster up the energy to take the babies with you, their tolerances are limited and it will result in a meltdown. If you keep your to-do list short, you and your children will be calmer.

GET OUT EVERY DAY!

Don't fall victim of house arrest. Just getting the troops out the door can be a handful, especially around everyone's diverse schedules of eating, pooping, and sleeping. But have a destination every day, even if it is only to run one quick errand or get mindlessly lost in Kmart.

Getting out of the house helps the babies too. A change in environment stimulates cognitive development even at a very young age.

TIP!

Hey! They get cabin fever too!

"Go out alone with your new children. Once you do, you will know that you can do it. Until then, you will feel trapped. You can still have a life, you'll just have a lot more company!"

—Bill and the Babies

"Try to get out every day with your babies. Don't believe you are a prisoner in your home just because you have triplets. You can do everything a person with one baby can. It just takes a little more planning."

—TG, Mentor, Ohio

RELAX YOUR HOUSEKEEPING STANDARDS

The action is non-stop in a house full of multiples, and you can expect less order, less privacy, and little to no personal time. Unless you have a housekeeper, routine household chores and maintenance will take a back seat to the babies' immediate back-to-back demands. For the neat freaks out there—accept it. The household chores will always be there, but your children won't.

TIP!

Who doesn't like fresh sheets and a sparkling kitchen? If you can afford a full-time housekeeper, great. If not, consider employing an occasional housekeeper. Maybe once a month, or every other month. This is a less expensive form of hired help than sitters or nannies, but it will give you relief in a different way.

"It was hard for me to relax my housekeeping and cooking, but I try to remember that taking care of three babies (and a ten-year-old) is a full-time job and the most important thing I can do."

—JJ, Bradenton, Fla.
The Triplet Connection

"It's OK if things aren't perfectly clean. Are your children smiling?"

—BT, N. Olmstead, Ohio

"I solved one problem by purchasing a shop vac. There is NOTHING it will not pick up, WET or DRY. I simply vacuum the high chairs and the kids before I let them out of their chairs. Once I purchased the shop vac, I started giving the kids things like RICE, which I would never do before. I have vacuumed up blobs of this and blobs of that—you name it. It really makes short work of meals and snacks."

—DF, Long Island, N.Y.

SHOWER

Take a shower every day. Not shower? How disgusting! Well, it happens. So make a pledge to yourself that you will work it in. You'll feel better, and look better too!

COLD MEALS

You will quickly learn that there is no such thing as a hot meal anymore, and it may be a long time before you can finish your now cold meal without being interrupted.

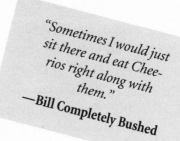

"Sometimes I would just sit there and eat Cheerios right along with them."

—Bill Completely Bushed

"Home in Babyland"—Surrendering Your Entire House to the Babies

When you hear one of them say *"uh-oh"* as the toilet is flushing, it's probably too late. Just when you thought you had made it through the zombie zone of sleepless nights, you will emerge into a new realm of challenges as they become increasingly mobile and curious. They will get into things you never knew you had. They will touch and taste everything, and wander into every nook and cranny of every room they are exposed to.

SAY "UNCLE"

There is no sense in fighting it. Surrender your entire house to them and create peace of mind for yourselves by baby-proofing every square inch the children will occupy.

- Give them plenty of safe space to roam, and turn them loose.
- Accept that your home will be cramped, cluttered, and filled with land mines of baby stuff.
- You won't win any home decorating awards, but you will have a little peace of mind, knowing that they are fairly safe.

TIP!

Silence does not necessarily mean "don't worry."

DO IT NOW, BEFORE THEY GET INTO EVERYTHING

Baby-proof everything before the children begin to crawl. Don't wait until they knock over your African violets and make sand castles out of the wet soil.

The days when they start bouncing off each other like feverish little molecules are just around the corner. It will be impossible to keep a watch on all of them simultaneously as they toddle off in different directions, exploring uncharted territory. Plus, multiples tend to put their little heads together and cook up ways to further their little discoveries and capers, including climbing on top of each other to reach higher surfaces.

TIP!

From this point forward it's Twin and Triplet Territory, Quad and Quint Country!

Knowing that they are safe will give you the peace of mind to enable you to leave the room, take a shower, cook a meal, or run to the bathroom without keeping a constant watch and constantly saying, "No!"

> *"They climbed every-thing. Keeping them safe... we limited their access to certain rooms and had extreme child-proofing in others."*
>
> —JB, **University Heights Ohio**

> *"I left the room for a few moments, came back, and Sabrina was on the buffet! There were two more sets of little eyes watching her with fascination. You could just see the little wheels turning inside their heads."*
>
> —Bill

If It's Really Treasured, Store It

A word of advice about your prized furnishings and possessions. Pack them away and kiss them good-bye for years.

- ❇ They will be spilled on, poured on, stuck on. They will be pulled on, pushed down, and jumped on.

- ❇ They will use furnishings as secret hiding places to stash their little treasures like animal crackers, Cheerios, and small toys.

> *"Whenever we are missing a sippy cup or a shoe, I always check the inside of the lower kitchen cupboards (which we had completely emptied, for their safety). I don't always find what I am looking for, but I always seem to find some other trinket of theirs stashed away. One day I found my own shoe in there!"*
>
> **—Sheila Searching for Buried Treasures**

Turn Rooms into Holding Pens

If you're completely out of space, turn your main living areas into the nursery. Where else do you put three cribs? This solution works for small apartments and when all bedrooms are occupied. It makes great sense for those who have too many stairs to climb. Remember what we said about saying "Uncle?"

> *"Establish a play area or playroom (if you have the room). Our dining room is now a playroom, we have nothing but toys in it and it is gated off at both entrances. This allows me to leave the room, do some laundry, clean the kitchen, make phone calls, all the while knowing the babies are completely safe in their playroom."*
>
> **—TG, Mentor, Ohio**

THE NO-FLY ZONE

> "Even when they're sick, we don't bring them into our bedroom to console them, because once you do that, they'll want to snuggle with Mommy and Daddy in the big bed all the time. Use a spare bedroom, living room, den, any separate area, but not your bedroom."
>
> —Bill Knows

We keep one area of the house off-limits to the children at all times and that is our bedroom. When our home became packed wall-to-wall with baby equipment, and the floors covered with crawling, drooling babies, there had to be one place we could go to reclaim some semblance of our adulthood. Our bedroom is our retreat: the one place in the house where we can get away when we need a break.

CREATIVE BABY-PROOFING TIPS FOR THE HANDY MAN

We recommend all the usual methods of baby-proofing such as, but not limited to, setting up gates, using door and drawer latches, removing plants and lamps that can be pulled down and knocked over, and removing the entire contents of lower cabinets. Yet, baby-proofing for multiples requires extra thought and caution. With so many babies and not enough sets of eyes, Bill found some creative measures that helped relieve the stress of trying to keep all the babies safe.

- **Tape Cords**—Tape electrical cords to furniture, walls, or floors to keep items from being pulled down.

- **Keep Venetian Blind Cords Rolled Up**—Venetian blind cords can be a dangerous strangulation hazard to small children. The cord roll-up devices that can be found at your local baby supply store are great, except for one thing: they can pop open after a while and release the cord. Solution— Drill a tiny hole in the dead center of it and put a small screw in it. Then wind up the cord as usual and screw the two pieces together and presto! No more resetting or rewinding again!

- ✛ **Box in the TV**—Build a box out of plywood that extends from the floor to the top of the TV and paint it black. Push the box against the wall and roll the TV, stand and all, into the box. Ta-dah! No cords to pull on or eat.

- ✛ **Bolt Furniture**—Where possible, bolt bookshelves and tall furniture to the walls. Multiples have a way of using each other to climb on top of things.

- ✛ **Double Gates**—With multiples, a single gate can be quickly conquered because they work together to make their escape. Install two gates in the same doorway.

- ✛ **Dutch Doors**—Replace regular doors in the center of the house with Dutch split doors.

- ✛ **Keep Kitchen Drawers Shut**—If you have the type of kitchen drawer handles that are shaped like a "U," baby-proofing all of them is easy. Measure from the top of the top handle to the floor, and then cut a one by two inch firing strip the same length. Screw a hook into one end of the strip. Slide the wooden strip down through the row of drawer handles like you were threading a needle. Once inserted, no drawer can be opened by itself because they're all connected by the wooden strip. Small children don't have the strength to open them all at once, nor are they tall enough to remove the wooden bar. Cost—under two bucks!

- ✛ **PVC Pipes**—Run PVC pipes through drawers that allow something to be pulled through them to prevent the children from using the drawers as steps to higher surfaces.

> *"Throw large bath towels over the tops of hallway and bedroom doors to prevent them from slamming on little fingers."*
>
> **— BL, Chagrin Falls, Ohio**

"Tools for the Job!"

WHO'S ON FIRST?

OK, you're exhausted. You've been at it for a while, everything is still a blur, and sometimes you mix up the babies. You're not alone.

Being a parent of multiples brings out your creativity. You start finding clever little tricks and techniques that you never knew you were capable of dreaming up, back in the days when you used to take a nice long hot baths or curl up with a good book.

For us, it all started like this... We were a couple of DINKs (Double Income, No Kids) who had transformed overnight into a couple of SINKS (that's Single Income, Numerous Kids). Before the babies, our house showed no signs of kids; you know, leather couches, off-white Berber carpet. Got the picture? We didn't even have an eat-in kitchen! We were faced with the question of what to do with three giant plastic high chairs holding three drooling, spoon-dropping, bowl-dumping, adorable babies sitting on a white Berber carpet in the middle of our dining room. So once again, Bill searched deep into the creative archives of his mind and cooked up another solution.

He built a temporary wooden floor that overlayed the carpet by taking a large sheet of plywood, painting it with polyurethane, and placing it under the high chairs. Our Uncle Russ (the dentist

> "Those singleton parents miss out on so much. Do they get to attempt to set the world record for days without consistent sleep? Do they get to confuse the identity of their own children in broad daylight when they are looking at them eye to eye?"
>
> —KT, Gilbert, Ariz.
> The Triplet Connection

in the family) gave us one of his examination stools with casters. And there it was! Back and forth we would scoot, chanting "*Feed, Feed, Feed, Wipe, Wipe, Wipe!*" Back and forth, back and forth. Hey, it worked!

Color-Code

Color-coding is a great way to keep the babies straight and determine who's been changed, fed, and given their goodnight kiss. It minimizes all the confusion of "who's who?" and "which baby didn't finish this bottle?"

- Permanently assign a color to each child, and apply it to everything you want to keep sorted. The children like it too!
- One Step Ahead makes a bottle collar that you can permanently write your baby's name on. It takes the guesswork out of whose bottle is whose, particularly if one is using a different formula than the others.
- Use different color markers or colored tape to differentiate.
- Color-code their medicine droppers to minimize confusion.

> *"We color-coded bottles, cups, cereal bowls, water bottles, toothbrushes, etc.... It helps me keep straight who is eating and drinking how much of what. But there are drawbacks; my son Owen says that his middle name is 'Blue.' Oh, well."*
>
> **—LL, Morrow, Ohio**

TIP!

Paint a Toenail! To keep from mixing them up, paint a toenail. Use two colors of nail polish if you have more than two identical babies.

Color-coding also helps when family and friends come over to help. Inevitably, they will ask, *"Whose bottle is this?"* and you'll likely say to yourself, *"Heck! I don't know!"* Color-coding the bottles will mean one less question that you have to answer. In your state of exhaustion, little things mean a whole lot.

> *"When the boys were infants, they looked so identical that we painted baby Austin's big toe nail red so we wouldn't mix them up and accidentally feed one of them twice and overlook the other."*
>
> **—Sheila and Bill**
> **Which Baby Are You?**

> *"Assign colors to the babies. We used red, green, and blue. I bought colored dots that stick and we used them to code bottles, vitamins, anything that needed to be kept separate. I still use the system today, marking shoes with colors to keep them sorted."*
>
> **—PA, The Triplet Connection**

FOOD PROCESSORS

Any food that is or can be cooked to a soft consistency and pureed is "baby food." The possibilities and choices are limitless.

> *"I make healthy, inexpensive, and appealing baby food by pureeing my own cooking, freezing it in ice cube trays, and storing it in Ziploc bags in the freezer. I mix their meat with yogurt or Ricotta cheese."*
>
> **—PS, Norwalk, Conn.**
> **The Triplet Connection**

BACKPACKS AND FANNYPACKS

These are great hands-free ideas to help you to get around town.

❌ Use fannypacks to store your keys and money when shopping. They stay secured to your body and you won't have the hassle of carrying a purse.

✖ Backpacks are a great alternative to the diaper bag. You can sling your arms through the straps and tote it along and keep your hands free for managing the crew.

Snaps and Zippers

Especially during the first six to twelve months, look for and ask for clothing with snaps or zippers. Trying to fasten eighteen to twenty-four buttons up the babies' backs in the middle of the night will put you over the edge. *No Buttons!* Snaps and zippers mean easy and quick access. One small detail in the deep of the night, with one baby down and two more to go, makes a huge difference. Save the fancier clothing with ties, bows, tights, and suspenders for company or special occasions.

"It seemed like our babies lived in their sleepers with snaps for the first nine months."
—Sheila

Label Shelves and Drawers

Organize clothing drawers or shelves by tops, bottoms, complete outfits, or by sex. Label the drawers or shelves accordingly. It's easier for you and for those who come in to lend a helping hand. They will be able to navigate around the nursery without any explanation.

Laundry Baskets

You're going to need a lot of them.

✖ Keep the babies' laundry separate from yours. That way, you won't find yourself at the office with a bad case of static cling and a couple of pink baby socks attached to your panty hose!

✖ Stay on top of it before it piles too high.

✖ If you have anything that has Velcro, attach it to its mate before throwing it in the wash, otherwise it sticks to everything.

✖ Keep a stain stick or a spray bottle of stain remover near the changing station (out of reach of course) and pre-treat spots before tossing the garment into the laundry basket.

> *"Keep the washing machine or a large pail always full of soap and water and stain cleaner. As soon as clothes or cloth diapers are changed, throw them in to soak. When it's full enough, go ahead and do a real wash. Stains are extremely reduced with virtually no effort."*
>
> **—DB, Puxico, Mo.**

 As a safety precaution, be sure to keep any open container out of reach of the children.

TUPPERWARE AND LARGE PLASTIC CONTAINERS

There are countless ways to use these containers.

✖ Plastic containers can keep the babies occupied for hours. They fill them and dump over and over again.

✖ Group toys by type, and store them in large containers. Blocks in one, toy cars in another. Eventually, teach the children to put one group of toys away before taking out another set.

✖ Crayons can be hard to put away in their original box, but not so with a Tupperware container.

✖ Empty a box of Cheerios into a large Tupperware-style container. You'll reach for these many times during the course of a day and this makes the access easy and saves time.

✖ Baby wipe containers can be reused to hold many small toys.

CLIPBOARDS, CALENDARS, AND JOURNALS

✖ Chart everything related to the babies' early progress. Even when someone comes to give you a helping hand, hand him or her the clipboard. Clipboards become the communication device between you and all of the people who come to help with the babies. It will help you keep

communication device between you and all of the people who come to help with the babies. It will help you keep track of all the babies' consumption and output and will make your visits to the pediatrician much less stressful.

✖ Calendars are critical tools for keeping schedules for hired and volunteer help and doctor's appointments. Keep them posted in a prominent place.

✖ As during pregnancy, a journal is a wonderful tool for recording your thoughts and feelings during parenthood.

✖ Write personal notes to your kids and stash them in their memory boxes.

> "I kept the paperback book that I read while on bedrest, and wrote a note to all my children and folded it inside the book. I told them what was going on in my life at the time I read it. Someday, they might read the very same book and get a peek of what life was like for me when I read it."
>
> —Sheila

Play-yards—"The OK Corral"

Traditional playpens are too small for your bunch. Play-yards are interlocking gates can be shaped into various forms, creating a play area that is much larger than a traditional playpen. Since they are bottomless, you may want to consider a blanket or sheet underneath, or go without, depending on the surface.

They are designed to collapse and fold up, so you can take them along while visiting or going to the park, and they keep your babies corralled.

Multitasking on the Telephone

You will receive a lot of phone calls (especially in the beginning) and Murphy's Law tells us they will come at the busiest times. You'll be in the middle of baths, diaper changes, crying episodes, or just plain exhaustion. Much like the strangers at the malls who want to know everything imaginable, your friends and family will break your stride by calling at the most inopportune time for the latest updates on you and the babes.

> *"Don't answer the phone if it's not convenient. I can't tell you how many times I wished that I hadn't answered the telephone when I had my hands full."*
>
> **—Bill**

- Voice mail or an answering machine will take the calls when you simply cannot get to the phone and will keep the interruptions to a minimum.
- Get caller ID.
- Better yet, get *Privacy Manger* by Ameritech.
- Let friends and relatives know the best times to call, such as during naps or after breakfast.

> TIP!
>
> **Ask them not to call during meals, bath time, or any other time you consider peak. This will help you finish the tasks at hand by minimizing the interruptions, and it prevents any potential alienation you may project.**

- Install phones (preferably cordless) in key locations such as the kitchen, changing stations, and the nursery (with the ringer turned off)—places where you will spend most of your time. That way if you're in the middle of feeding, or changing a diaper or two or three (which we always are), you can answer the phone and talk while attending to baby business.

> *"Do you know how many times I've had two little feet in the air and a dirty wipe in the other hand, and Jo Schmo is calling to sell me waterproofing? Privacy Manager requires the caller to identify himself, giving you the choice of taking the call or letting the service take the call. That way if it's your overdue babysitter calling from a pay phone, you can grab it. If it's Joe Schmo again, just press one button and the service tells him to remove you from his calling list, and you can go back to your own little waterproofing job."*
>
> **—Bill and the Babies**

"Separation Anxiety"—Balancing Your Career and Multiples

Finding the right balance between career commitments and family commitments is difficult, not to mention the difficulty of having enough energy left over to truly enjoy each child and spend quality time with your partner.

> *"In the blink of an eye, I can transform from the professional in a tailored red gabardine wool suit to the housewife in a T-shirt and ponytail, on her hands and knees mopping up spills and wiping butts and noses. After all, working mothers of multiples have it all, don't they? They have long hard hours, overnight business travel, deadlines, and quotas to meet. They have multiple tasks and countless demands from multiple babies when they get home. My family comes first, my career a very close second."*
>
> **—Sheila, Mother and Career Woman**

STAY ONE STEP AHEAD

As a working parent of multiples, there will be mornings you will feel all used up even before you leave the house. To head this off, prepare for the next day the night before.

TIP!

A ten-minute prep the night before can save thirty minutes tomorrow morning.

❖ Select your clothes the night before—down to the last detail. Have your briefcase packed and ready to go, sitting by the door.

❖ Know where your car keys are.

❖ Before bed, pull tomorrow's dinner out of the freezer.

❖ Pour and cap bottles or sippy cups with milk or juice the night before.

❖ Make your list of things to-do and remember, keep it short! You aren't likely to get it all done.

❖ Don't let the laundry pile up.

❖ Line up next week's help schedule.

None of these activities by themselves are very time-consuming. It's when you try doing them in the same hour that you are trying to attend to the rise-and-shine morning drill and get out the door to work that it can become very stressful.

DECIDING NOT TO GO BACK TO WORK

"Family first, careers second. Your children are first forever."
—BT, N. Olmstead, Ohio

If you are thinking that you might be bored staying at home all day long with kids, or if you envision lots of spare time to pursue personal interests, think again. The opposite is true, you will have little to no free time, and all your needs and special interests seem to vaporize into thin air!

> **TIP!**
>
> **Your work day will change from eight hours a day to twenty-four. Your work week goes from five days to seven. You get no sick days, no personal days, and no vacation days.**

Parents of multiples may work harder at home than they would at the office, yet many of those who stay home with their children recognize the importance of their role and are proud to provide a quality life for their family.

> *"My career is my family. I have no guilt."*
> —JB, University Heights, Ohio

> *"Fortunately, my kids are my career."*
> —KD, N.Olmstead, Ohio

"Parenting Is a Team Sport"—Co-Parenting

The literature needs to be rewritten. It is hard to believe, but our society still draws a distinction between the roles of the mother and the father. Child care literature is, amazingly, still all directed to MOM. This attitude is validated everywhere you turn, in books, magazines, advertisements, and even the way our health benefits are structured. It is still only the more forward-thinking companies that offer paternity leave. Especially in families with multiple birth children, fathers are sharing more and more of the responsibility of child care and housekeeping chores.

Multiples means multiple commitments from both parents—Mom and Dad!

With multiples, duties become gender-free. Even the most conservative families will find themselves breaking tradition as they share in the responsibilities. It's not role reversal, it's role sharing.

Heavy involvement from both parents is a win-win combination for both parents and the children. Here are some ways to ease into it.

"Jay never missed a beat. You should see him with our babies!"
—NJ, Macedonia, Ohio

"Mike got right in there; he even changes diapers on airplanes."
—MH, Lakewood, Ohio

"We fathers learn that all dirty diapers are delegated to us, and that eighteen to twenty-five changes a day invokes the 'practice makes perfect' theory. We relish in wrapping the 'spent' diapers and tossing them clear across the room to make two points into the receptacle."

—KT, Gilbert, Ariz.
The Triplet Connection

DON'T KEEP SCORE

Strike a balance that works for your family. If he likes to do the cooking and you don't mind the laundry, then so be it. If you approach the unending tasks in partnership, you will find that it all works out fairly evenly by the end of the day. And if it doesn't, that's OK.

ON DUTY/OFF DUTY

There will be times when one of you pulls a heavier shift than the other, but what goes around will likely come around. When one needs a break or wants to step out of the ring for a while, take turns being on duty. Agree on how long the other is "off." It could be thirty minutes, two hours, a morning, or an afternoon. Let your partner have their own personal adult time to do whatever they please. Your turn is next!

> *"As soon as we heard the first of the morning's babbling, I would rise and quickly shower. Next, I set up breakfast, assembly-line style—high chairs, bibs, bottles, cereal, spoons, etc., and of course, not forgetting the dog and all of his needs. Then I would make my entrance into the nursery to greet my three smiling little ones and all their diapers. About this time Bill would rise, shower, and join us, taking over. As he fed the babies, I would dress and make my way out of the house. This was a good balance, since I got to enjoy the babies in the morning while it gave Bill a break, since he would be on triple duty until I came home."*
>
> **—Sheila in the Shuffle**

MAKE A FRONT LINE PACT

When the situation gets tense (and it will), and you are starting to snap at each other, have an agreement that the one who's "losing it" walks away—leaves the room, takes a walk outside, or simply leaves the front line.

STAY FLEXIBLE

One of the most important jobs in life is parenting, and with multiples the job becomes enormous. You and your partner will not always agree on how to manage and raise the children. The disagreements will intensify the stress level, especially if it comes during fussing and crying episodes. Recognize it for what it is, and see to the babies' needs. When things settle down, talk about it. You need each other more than ever now, and you must be flexible and willing to compromise.

Stay-at-Home Dads

Today's western society is taking some of the largest strides ever in the area of family relationships. These strides involve a re-examination of male and female roles with regard to raising children, and the recognition of family management as a legitimate career choice for both men and women. For some families, like ours, it meant a decision to adopt, at least temporarily, a lifestyle in which Dad stays at home and cares for the children while Mom pursues a career.

When we decided that Bill would stay home with our three babies while I returned to work, we soon became aware of just how far society still has to go in preparing for, accepting, and affirming the contributions of a stay-at-home dad. Society generally considers being a homemaker as an acceptable career choice for women if the family can afford it. We have found that society (with few exceptions) does not view a man in the same light.

Before people know our situation they *always*, without exception, think I am helping out my wife. Typical comments from strangers include:

❈   "Triplets! Your poor wife!"—while I am pushing them in a stroller and pulling a shopping cart alone.

❈   "Triplets! How does your wife do it? She must be pretty busy."

❈   "It's so nice of you to give your wife a break, not many men would do that."

❈   "Where is your wife?"—as they look over my shoulder.

❈   "How sweet. Daddy is taking the kids out to lunch."

When someone finds out that Bill is a stay-at-home dad, they almost always offer an incredulous re-statement of the fact, followed by a slightly condescending statement, as if granting their permission for this unorthodox arrangement. Responses include:

- "Wow! You're kidding. I think that's great!"
- "That's great, you don't have to work. HA! HA!"
- "Man, you've got guts."
- "More men should try it. Really, I mean it."
- "Isn't that neat."

And then, there are the responses that indicate concern. It seems some people believe that Bill was forced into this position due to a temporary financial setback, a wife with an extraordinarily high-paying career, or some other unusual set of circumstances. They say things like:

- "No kidding. Your wife must do pretty well. What does she do?"
- "That's really something. When will you be going back to work?"
- "How did *you* end up staying home with the kids?"
- "Do you think you will stay at home long?"
- Children have quizzed Bill, "How come? Why don't you work?" and really ignorant people have asked, "How does it feel to be a mom?"

"I hate that one! I do not consider myself 'Mr. Mom' any more than Sheila considers herself 'Mrs. Dad.' That term in my mind is so old and outdated. The best advice we can give anyone is just keep smiling and consider the good intentions behind the comments."

—Bill

Society has changed over the years, but it still has a long way to go before a man can say he is a stay-at-home dad without anyone blinking an eye.

> *TIP!*
>
> **Even the multiple birth support organizations are directed at mothers, even using "Moms" or "Mothers" in their names. But they too have started to recognize the growing number of involved fathers. They are now describing themselves as support groups for *parents* rather than just moms, and are including columns and articles in their publications written by fathers.**

Men, who have been socialized to believe they should be out in the world bringing home the bacon, may sometimes feel that they have made a wrong turn somewhere. Emotionally, we can't help being influenced by society, no matter how committed we are to our decision.

Bill and our children have been involved in a couple of local support groups. They get together for play groups and other social functions geared around the children.

> *"My mind tells me that all the logical factors that influenced my wife and me in this decision were correct. My mind tells me we are doing the right thing and made the right choice. My mind tells me that what I am doing is extremely important and will directly affect my children: their development, success, and happiness. Yet, when I go to a friend's house to watch a football game, and all my buddies are talking about work, deals, associates, and the 'outside world'—I question my decision. My world is now my house and my children. At first, my job seemed small and unimportant, and I felt the need to justify my situation to others. As time goes on, these feelings grow smaller and smaller. I feel better and better about my chosen path. When someone says how wonderful my children are I feel proud, and I am sure that being a stay-at-home dad, helping my children grow and develop with love, was the right choice. It is the best thing that ever happened to me!"*
>
> —Bill, a Proud Stay-at-Home Dad

Bill says he and the children have gotten a great deal out of being involved with these groups, though he still doesn't feel comfortable going to a "Mom's night out."

STAY-AT-HOME DAD'S JOB DESCRIPTION

"As the only man, it took a little while before I felt as if I fit in, especially when the conversation was about carrying the babies, childbirth, or breastfeeding. Once they got past that, it was smooth sailing."

—Bill

From birth to around four months, it's a twenty-four hours a day, seven days a week schedule. At around four months, the children begin to sleep through the night and you only have to work twelve hours a day, seven days a week, with no sick days, no personal days, no weekends, no vacations, and no pay. As the children get older, the job of being a stay-at-home dad seems to get easier, even though we are really swapping one task for another as the children develop and grow. Add to the job description home maintenance chores like plumbing, roofing, furniture repair, painting, landscaping, and all the other "weekend warrior" tasks most men do.

TIP!

But Wait! There is one thing that makes this job different than others, something that makes you want to work long hours with no pay. That is the people you work with: your own children. Every day you can count on something amazing: an expression that catches you off guard, a small little something they learned, a tender moment, or just looking at them and realizing that they are turning from infants to children—real people. These things can't be found or duplicated in any other job.

"I have never worked so hard, so many hours, for so little pay, and loved it so much!"

—Bill

Dear Human Resources Department,

If you are interested in an employee who can perform multiple tasks, manage a tight budget, skillfully resolve conflicts, function well with little sleep, work well under pressure, lead by example, stay until the job is done, juggle multiple schedules, and handle very tough situations with ease, then consider a parent of Supertwins. After all, after surviving the first two years with multiples, any difficult challenge you may have in store for them will seem trivial.

—Kyle and Crew, Gilbert, Ariz.

Chapter Five

"Are They Natural?"

The public is fascinated by multiples. As you navigate your way through stores and parking lots, the babies leave ripples of wonder in their wake. Interestingly, the general public somehow believes it is their right to know everything, and *we mean everything!*

"Nothing Is Off-Limits"—Personal Questions from Nosy People and Complete Strangers

You will be pointed at and whispered about. Perfect strangers will stop you dead in your tracks and stand staring before your stroller. Less aggressive ones will wait on the fringes until you stop in a shopping aisle to select an item off the shelf, or until you have your hands completely full loading or unloading the babies, and then *Bam!* You're a sitting duck and, presumably, fair game for any and all intrusive and personal questions including *how* you became pregnant, *what* is your sex life like, and *what* was your fertility history. They want to know how you *stayed* pregnant, what the delivery was like, how do you breastfeed all of them and "*how in the h… do you do it?*"

Two of my favorite personal examples of the public's behavior:

> *"I was on an airplane and the flight attendant noticed me looking at some photos of my children. Now picture this: everyone was seated, and all eyes were on the stewardess with the beverage cart. 'Oh! Triplets! Hey, everyone, she has triplets!' Then she held up pictures of my babies. 'Are they natural? Did you take fertility drugs? How is it done, I mean come on, what does the man have to do (tee-hee)? Did you have a Cesarean?'" Thanks.*

> *"I was in New York City on business, and was having some hors d'oeuvres at the hotel. A woman approached me and asked to share my table. At some point in the ensuing conversation, I told her I had just finished shopping for my children. 'Oh, how old are your children?' 'Thirteen months,' I replied. 'Twins?' 'Actually, we have triplets.' 'God bless you and congratulations,' she said. Her husband joined us, and she joyfully told him that I am the mother of triplets. The conversation turned back to shopping. 'So what did you buy for your children?' she asked. Her husband quickly interrupted her and said, 'Honey I think that's by far too personal a question; so tell me, was this an assisted reproduction?'" True story.*

> —Sheila

COPING STRATEGIES!

BE PREPARED

People's questions and comments are sometimes so outrageous that they can catch you off guard, put you on the defensive, or make you lose your temper. Anticipating their questions and having a few snappy comebacks on the tip of your tongue can help you take nosy people in stride and still enjoy your outing.

> *"I still get angry about what some people say. I know it's not worth it, but I do. Most of the time I have a canned answer for the usual questions. 'Multiples run in the family.' 'No, they don't all cry at the same time.' 'I'm glad it's me and not you, too.'"*
>
> **—NJ, Macedonia, Ohio**

MAINTAIN YOUR SENSE OF HUMOR

Give people the benefit of the doubt. Most people don't have a clue about how rude or offensive their questions can be. They see your children as a miracle that needs explaining. But remember, you have a right to protect your family's privacy, and just because a question is asked doesn't mean you must answer it.

> *"I get a kick out of the silly questions like, 'Are those all yours?' or 'I bet they keep you busy, huh?' I relish the opportunity to say, 'No, not really. Nope. I just borrow this silly locomotive-like stroller and see how long they last before one of them screams at fifty decibels due to a dirty diaper.'"*
>
> **—KT, Gilbert, Ariz.**
> **The Triplet Connection**

HOW DID THIS HAPPEN?

One subject that seems to hold an especially strong interest for the general public is the question of how multiples are conceived. People's fascination and insensitive quest for personal details about *how* you became pregnant is insatiable, and they often demand an explanation.

For parents who conceived through assisted reproduction, personal questions about their babies' conception can be particularly disturbing. Couples usually turn to fertility treatment after they have exhausted all other avenues of conception and possibly faced many lost pregnancies. They have dealt with the dreaded invitations to baby showers, feelings of inadequacy, and acts of denial. They have ridden emotional roller coasters, faced enormous medical expenses, and more likely than not failed again and again at conception.

People who receive fertility treatment have a medical problem. Not unlike a patient with kidney failure or diabetes, they have a bodily function that isn't working. Yet the general public, encouraged by sensationalized TV shows and articles, believes they have the right to know all the details of your case. The fact that sex is involved only serves to intensify the level of intrigue.

TIP!

It is amazing how knowledgeable the public *thinks* they are on the subject of multiples.

The public clings to the notion that you pop a few fertility drugs and immediately become pregnant with multiples. I was once asked, "Did you use fertilizer?" The sobering fact is "high-tech science fails three of four infertile couples."[*]

Here are a few classic questions and comments that you will field, along with some suggested responses.

"Are they natural?"	"Yes, all of them," and push on.
	"Nope, they're man-made," and keep on truckin.'
"Did you take fertility drugs?"	"Yes, but I didn't inhale."
	"Just ate a lot of bananas."
	"God gave us a miracle."
	"No."
"You didn't do that on your own, did you?"	"It took three storks!"
	"My wife/husband helped."
"Did you have to 'do it' three times?"	"I'd like to get the details on your sex life before I answer that, but first, who are you?"
	Raise your head up high and proud. Then say, "No, just three times better than you'll ever know."

Newsweek, "Has the Hype Outweighed the Hope?" 1995.

"You didn't, ahm, breastfeed, did you (tee-hee)?"

Not even worth responding to.

"You didn't deliver vaginally, did you?"

"Excuse me, but... do I know you?"

"How much weight did you gain?"

"Plenty."

"Well within the required amount, thank you."

"How Do You Do It?"

The public is also fascinated by the concept of caring for so many babies. While often meant to express awe and admiration, their comments can be insulting, discouraging, and unsupportive, depending on your mood at the time. Total strangers will shake their heads and say, "How do you do it?" or "Better you than me." Concerned passersby will ask if you have had your tubes tied or counsel you to be careful what you wish for.

"The most outrageous comment D. and I ever got was from a lady who came up to us, looked at me and said, 'I'm glad he's sleeping with you and not me!' I told her, 'I bet he is too!'"

—JB, University Heights, Ohio

Again, we offer a few classic comments along with suggested responses:

"I bet you have your hands full."

"Yes, full of love."
"Double work but triple the treat."

"I can't imagine! How do you do it?"

"It's easy. We're excellent parents!"
"The same way you do, it just takes a little longer."
"The best we can."

"You poor thing."
"I thought I had it bad."

"We've been blessed."
"These babies are so special. I wouldn't trade them for the world."
"From the looks of you, you do."

"I'm glad it's you,   "Me too."
not me."
                            "So are we."

"Better you than me."   "I agree."

It can be tedious, when you are trying to accomplish errands on a tight schedule, to answer the same questions over and over.

TIP!

Our best advice is to keep on walking.

If possible, take someone with you—your spouse, a sitter, or a friend—and two strollers. With twins, put one baby in each stroller; with triplets, put two babies in one twin stroller and the third in a single or umbrella stroller. A set of twins and a singleton will draw significantly less attention and you can get your business done with little distraction.

"If people insist on probing, they will have to keep up with you."
—Blazin' Bill and the Babies

We sometimes will take the triplet stroller and let the sitter stroll around the store with the babies while we concentrate on finding the best priced diapers and formula.

More examples of common questions and suggested responses:

"Are those really twins,   Smile and say, "No, they're cousins."
triplets, quads?"
                                  Smile and say, " Oh no, they're just day care kids."

"Who is the smartest of the   "They're all special."
bunch, the instigator, the
leader? Who is your   "We love them all."
favorite?" (**Children are
not immune to these kinds
of questions.**)

When all else fails, or when you are caught off-guard by a personal or intrusive question from a stranger… stop!… pause, look directly in their eyes, and politely ask, "Do I know you?"

"Asking someone who has multiples, 'Are these all yours?' is like asking someone, 'Are all those your real teeth?'"

—Kyle and Crew, Ariz.

Of course, there will be times when you and the babies will revel in the attention being lavished on you. On any outing, you can usually count on at least one or two people to remind you of how blessed you are. You'll hear comments like:

"They're gorgeous!"	Eat it up!
"God has blessed you!"	Marvel in the glory!
"How lucky you are!"	Take it all in!

Three years later, it still hasn't stopped.

TIP! The best strategy for coping with such comments is to smile and let it go. Otherwise you could impede the sharing and the empathy of parenting in general and potentially alienate other parents.

"OH, I HAD TWO BABIES IN DIAPERS AT ONE TIME..."

Parents of singletons often try to compare their hardships of raising two or more singletons in close succession to your unique experience of raising multiples. Even parents of twins compare their hardships to those of triplet parents, and up the line it goes. With each additional baby added to the mix, the complexity and dynamics change exponentially. Until they walk in your shoes, they will never really know.

"I laugh when I see those singleton parents who look like sleep-deprived marathon runners with one child in their grocery cart."

—KT, Gilbert, Ariz.
The Triplet Connection

"I have found that I have to ignore the advice of well-meaning relatives and their friends concerning how to handle my children. Triplets are NOT the same as having three children in close succession."

—PA, The Triplet Connection

Chapter Six

"Bringing Home the Bacon"—
Financial Issues

While co-workers are out buying a new pair of shoes, one in navy, one in black, and one in brown, we're out buying cases of diapers and wipes.

"There's a Hole in My Pocket"—Creating a Financial Safety Net for Their Future

There are going to be more expenses than your can even imagine. In the early years, you will spend tons of money on baby equipment, food, and supplies. Then there will come a day when you will be paying for soccer camps, basketball uniforms, computers, braces, and who knows what else. Children cost money, lots of money.

> **TIP!**
>
> **Would you believe children cost $1,455,581 apiece? And yes, girls cost 18 percent more than boys.**

"You start to look at life a little differently when diaper sales and baby food coupons make your hair stand up on the back of your neck. You know, the way it did when you got your new 'vette, which has since been financially altered into cribs, changing tables, high chairs, mobiles, car seats, blankets, cool mist vaporizers, and a stroller that takes thirty-seven steps and five minutes to assemble and disassemble; and you'll have more co-pays than NHL games you will miss in the first two years."

—KT, Gilbert, Ariz.
The Triplet Connection

U.S. News & World Report added up as best it can all the costs of raising a child from birth to college graduation. They utilized data from the U.S. Department of Agriculture (USDA), which estimates how much families of various income brackets spend on raising a child to the age of eighteen. They then added the costs of a college education and "wages foregone due to the rigors of child-rearing" and it comes out to a whopping 1.45 million dollars. ***Each.*** That's right, each. According to the USDA, just to clothe a child to age eighteen averages a small fortune: $22,063.*

The financial sacrifice that you will make for your multiples over the next twenty-two years is just now beginning. Unlike singletons who are born in succession, multiples don't hand down equipment and clothing to each other.

Of course there is more to life than just money, but you're going to need a lot of it for a very long period of time. So here are some tactics to help get you started on creating a financial safety net for their future and yours.

SET UP A MUTUAL FUND FOR EACH CHILD

It's easier than you think! Set up a fund for each child each starting with $100 each. If you add $100 every birthday to each fund, and assume an average rate of return of 8 percent, by age twenty-one they will have over $5,500 per account. But $5,500 isn't enough!

By the time they reach age twenty-one that will be enough money to cover the sales tax on a dinner and a movie!!

---

*U.S. News & World Report, March 30, 1998.

If you start with $100 dollars per fund and add $100 *each month*, at an average rate of return of 8 percent, it will amount to over $45,000 by age eighteen per account, and $61,000 after twenty-one years.

And these are very conservative estimates. Chances are very good that you can achieve a much higher rate of return than 8 percent.

T!P!

The secret is getting started *now* and letting time and interest rates do their compounding magic!

Now, remember what we said about your lifestyle changing forever?

Eliminate the Nonessential

First, find out where the money is going. If you have never done this, open up your checkbook and get out a BIG piece of paper. Create columns for household expenses (rent, mortgage, utilities, food), car expenses (car payment, gas, repairs, car washes), insurance (car, home, medical, life), credit cards, medical, savings, and miscellaneous expenses.

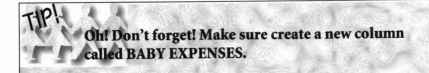

T!P!

Oh! Don't forget! Make sure create a new column called BABY EXPENSES.

Now, get out a big box of Kleenex and start scrolling through your checkbook. Plug all of your expenses into the above categories. And don't forget the "mad money" you burn through every day on who knows what!! Highlight the categories that are essential to living, such as keeping a roof over your head, food on the table, *and, of course, diapers*. Weigh this against your monthly after tax income, and now you'll know. If you've never done this exercise before, it can be pretty pitiful.

We should have listened to our mothers when they said, *"Save it for a rainy day,"* but it's never too late to get a grip on your finances. You don't have to lower your standard of living, just simplify it and manage your money a little better with some frugal tactics.

To simplify things, start with:

❖ Automatic direct deposit for your paychecks.

❖ Arrange for automatic deduction from your checking account for car payments, utility bills, and your mortgage. Using this payment method takes away the routine hassle of writing another check, addressing another envelope, and getting it into the mail with a stamp on it. We're always running out of stamps, and who wants to spend their valuable time standing in line at the friendly local post office?

❖ Shop online—it takes away the hassles that go along with shopping at the mall.

"Make Every Penny Count!" Money-Saving Tips!

Every little bit helps! Here are some ideas for saving money:

❖ Borrow whatever baby items you can.

❖ Don't buy name-brand diapers. They will take your budget right down the toilet!

❖ Give haircuts at home.

❖ Eliminate cable TV and stick with the basic channels. Besides, most of the time it will be tuned into *Barney, Teletubbies,* or *Sesame Street.*

❖ Borrow videos from your local library. They usually have a good selection and they're free!!

- Eat at home. You're a much better cook than you think. Plus, it's fun concocting meals for your little ones.
- When you go out for a meal, find the restaurants where kids eat free.
- Send e-mail instead of calling long distance.
- Shop at half-price or close-out stores.
- Buy generic medicines at the pharmacy, if available.
- Buy the local store's equivalent brand of over-the-counter medicine and cold remedies. They usually have exactly the same ingredients and are much less expensive. Read the labels!
- Don't buy name brand make-up at department stores—no one will know.
- Join SAM's Club (or other bulk retailer) and buy in bulk.
- Watch the ads at the grocery store and buy what's on sale.
- Watch for rebates.
- Dollar stores are filled with too many items to list. They are packed with good stuff.
- Pack your lunch, if appropriate.
- Cancel magazine subscriptions—when was the last time you had time to read them?
- If you work and have good benefits, go on disability when you are pregnant and let a portion of your salary roll in.
- Do as many free things as possible. Attend play groups for multiples. Don't forget about your local parks.
- Read *The Millionaire Next Door* by Thomas J. Stanley and William D. Danko.

Saving Money on Supplies

Add in all the other baby stuff and look out! *Ouch!!* Here are some ideas that can help. Each one by itself may not add up to a big chunk of change, but over time it can make a difference.

> **TIP!** Between disposable diapers and baby formula, you can expect to spend over four thousand after-tax dollars *the first year!*

FREE FORMULA!

We can't say exactly what you will spend on formula the first year. It depends on how much help you get from manufacturers, store sales, any needs for special formula, and of course, your children's appetite. We found that our triplets went through about one can of powdered formula per day from around the age of three months to one year. Formula costs roughly $10 per can or $2,750 the first year. If you purchase by the case and use coupons, you can get the formula expense down to about $2,550 the first year.

Have your pediatrician contact his or her local formula representative. The representatives are often sympathetic and generous, and willing to donate a limited supply. Usually your pediatrician will load you up with whatever supply they have on hand during each visit.

> **TIP!** *Don't Forget to Say Thanks!* We wrote a thank you note to our pediatrician's formula rep (who we had never met) who came through for us with cases and cases of formula. We left the note at our pediatrician's office for him to pick up on his next sales call. Six weeks later, he showed up on our doorstep and hand-delivered three more cases! *Thanks, Joe!*

SAVE 80 PERCENT ON BABY WIPES!

I don't know about you, but we *hate* spending money on things that we use once and throw away. The disposable diapers are bad enough, but baby wipes take first prize—*what a price racket!* It is fast and easy to make your own, and they are just as good and just as disposable as the packaged ones off the shelf.

> *"Take a stack of paper towels, cut them in half, put them in a Tupperware container, add a mixture of one cup water and two tablespoons of baby oil, and you have homemade baby wipes that cost forty cents instead of three dollars."*
>
> —GW, Fairfield, Calif.

TIP!

Hey! Why not use an old baby wipes container to store your own!!

COUPONS

Clip and collect them. Enlist your friends, family, and sitters to save coupons for you. You'll find them for diapers, wipes, and many other baby supplies. For an added bonus, use your coupons when the items go on sale, and you can reduce your costs on supplies by up to 35 percent.

> *"My wife and I use an electric knife to cut our store-bought wipes in half since babies' bottoms are so small. They go a lot farther when you cut them in half."*
>
> —RMS, Ohio

GARAGE SALES AND CHURCH SALES

Resale shops, garage sales, and church rummage sales are excellent places to find gently used baby equipment, clothing, and toys.

- ❖ If it can be cleaned and is in good condition, buy it! You will save a small fortune. You can use the money for diapers.

- ❖ When shopping at garage sales, tell them you have multiples—it helps!

- ❖ Do the same at a retail store.

"Triplet Mom Selling Three of Everything!"

❖ Save all your baby equipment and clothing as the children outgrow them, and then hold your own garage sale.

❖ Advertise in your local paper "Triplet Mom Selling Three of Everything" and people will line up down the driveway.

❖ What does not sell, save for your next sale or donate to charity.

> *"Start buying little nothing toys at garage sales even before they are born, and don't pay more than a quarter! Your children will find any new toy interesting. With a pile of inexpensive little toys, you can introduce a few at a time, rotating the toys whenever the children get bored with them. All for just a few bucks."*
>
> **—Bargain Bill**

> *"Do you know how much one good pair of leather baby shoes cost?? When she saw all of us together, the lady gave me a bag and said, 'fill it up with as many pairs of shoes as it will hold and call it two bucks!'"*
>
> **—Shopping with Sheila**

Buy Off-Season

If you shop retail for new clothing, buy larger sizes that will fit them when next year rolls around at today's "end-of-the season" sale prices. This can mean a savings of 50 to 75 percent off list! Exchange the many newborn outfits you receive for larger-size clothing during off-season sales.

BABY FOOD

Most foods that can be cooked, pureed, and strained are baby food. Purchase baby food by the case when on sale. It pays to talk to the store manager for an additional discount on each case since the store does not have to stock it.

> *"Those singleton parents, they miss out on so much. It's amazing how long it takes to a store clerk to ring up two hundred and fifty small baby food jars."*
>
> —KT, Gilbert, Ariz.
> The Triplet Connection

OUTLET STORES

Outlet stores are great places to save on clothing. Their merchandise is often "irregular or imperfect" but it usually is pretty good stuff.

CONSIGNMENT STORES

Shop and sell in the baby consignment stores and you'll save a small fortune. They generally have high-quality standards for merchandise they will take, which means the clothing and equipment is gently used. If you have items that "make the grade" they usually offer you cash on the spot, and sometimes they will pay more than what you'd get if you sold it at a garage sale.

SWAP MEETS FOR MULTIPLES

Many multiples clubs and twins clubs organize sales once or twice a year. These sales are great places to find used baby equipment and nearly new matching or coordinating outfits.

> *"At one point, we had enough diapers to line the Great Wall of China, and then one day they were all gone."*
>
> —Sheila

> *"We also buy in bulk when diapers are on sale. I think at one point we had about 400 diapers on hand."*
>
> —RMS, Ohio

STOCK UP!

When you see diapers and supplies on sale, stock up. Don't worry about not using them up, because you will.

DON'T SKIMP ON SOME THINGS

The old cliché, "you get what you pay for," applies to safety items, dishwasher detergent, and laundry detergent. If you use discount detergent, you'll end up washing laundry at least twice to get it clean.

"You guys told us to ask our local grocer for discounts, so we did. Anytime they have a sale on baby stuff, I buy a bunch and they give me rain checks for a bunch more for the future."

—NJ, Macedonia, Ohio

TIP!

Stay connected with your local retailers. They will often extend sale prices for you, or even call you when items are about to go on sale.

"It's Only Eighteen Years Away"— Starting a College Fund

You have probably already started thinking about their future, more specifically, college. You've probably asked yourself more than once, "How are we going to afford it for two or three or four all at the same time?"

Who wants their kids flipping burgers for a living? We say, start a college fund NOW! Immediately! It doesn't matter how much money you don't make or don't have.

"Let's see, how much does it cost to take a family of five to the ballpark? How about that car insurance? Since they give diaper coupons to parents of multiples, I'm sure they offer some type of multi-user discount for college tuition, you think?"

—KT, Gilbert, Ariz.
The Triplet Connection

The act of setting aside a consistent amount on a regular basis is the key. Time and compounded interest will take care of the rest.

It can be structured once a week, once a month, once every paycheck. Regard the act of setting aside money for college the same way you regard paying the rent, the mortgage, or a utility bill. Just do it!

"BUT I DON'T HAVE ANY EXTRA MONEY"

Yes, you do. Heck, we bet you spend $100 a month on stuff you can't even account for. This is your children's opportunity for a good future, my friend, so reach into your pocket, scrape up the dough, and get started.

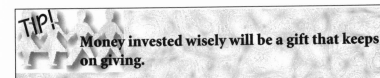

TIP! Money invested wisely will be a gift that keeps on giving.

WHERE TO BEGIN

Consider the following strategies for scraping up some extra cash:

- ❖ Use any gift money they receive when they are born as starter funds. Channel all other gift money from birthdays, holidays, etc. into their funds. It all adds up.

- ❖ Take a couple of old baby bottles, one for each child, and throw your loose change into them. When the bottles fill up, deposit the money into their college fund.

- ❖ Once they are potty trained, take the money you were spending each month on diapers and write a check for that amount each month and put it in the college fund. You'll never miss the money!

FINANCIAL AID

When the time comes, there are a multitude of financial aid sources. Some potential sources are: federal loans, federal grants, state sources, private sources, employer plans, tax credits, military programs, Veterans Administration programs, cooperative education, and colleges themselves.

You may be surprised at what you qualify for, especially with multiple children attending college simultaneously. Some colleges offer "sibling discounts," not necessarily for twins, triplets, and more, but a reduced rate for siblings attending college at the same time.

TIP!

Don't rule anything out because you think you earn too much, or saved too much, or the college is too expensive, or your children don't have the grades. Learn the facts while your children are still young, and you have time to position your finances properly and begin an appropriate savings program based on your projected college needs.

Most people don't take the time to learn what is available. They want a quick answer and blindly fill out a few forms at the school office, missing many possible opportunities for aid. Most do not know where to get information to make the right decisions and choices. It is important to take the time to learn how financial aid really works.

On the surface, financial aid seems too complex for lay people like us to understand. It certainly is too large a topic to cover in this book; however, there are quite a few books that can help. One book we think is particularly good is *Don't Miss Out* by Anna and Robert Leider. It explains the various forms of aid and has worksheets to help determine what your expected family contribution should be, based on the most recent financial aid programs available today. There is even software designed to run "what if" models with your expected family contribution. See Chapter 14 for where to get this information.

Programs change, therefore it is important to get a head start on understanding and planning for college now and to periodically look for new changes in laws and programs, especially as your children near college age.

Remember, your multiple blessings may open multiple doors to financial aid.

"Does This Make Sense?" Day Care—Evaluating Your Decision and the Center

All parents worry when it comes to leaving their children and relying on others for their safety and protection. There are no easy answers. We found many parents of multiples take a strong position, either "for it" or "against it." Putting your philosophies aside, some parents have to return to work just to make ends meet. Others want to return to work and continue their careers.

"I love my job. I need a balance in my life between the outside adult world and my family. This way, I appreciate and enjoy my children much more."

—Triplet Mom, San Francisco, Calif.

"Totally against it. You are and always will be the best parent for your children."

—JB, University Heights, Ohio

"I'm for it. We use day care on occasion. It gives us a much-needed break, and it gives the children more socialization exposure than we can provide."

—Sheila

"It scares me. If I could find an affordable day care that I truly felt was good, I think it would be an excellent idea on a part-time basis. Not only do the parents obviously need a break, but also, I think the children need to learn social interaction with other children. My three developed their own style of talking, playing, and fighting together, but they had no other children around to learn other social interactions."

—DB, Puxico, Mo.

"Work nights."

—BT, N. Olmstead, Ohio

If you are considering day care centers, we recommend the following approach, which may ease some of your concerns. This approach will help you gather the information you need to make a good decision up front, before you make a commitment.

THE COSTS

Evaluate the cost and weigh it against your income potential. Unless you have a great-paying job, day care for multiples may not even be an option. Depending on how reputable the center is and what area of the country, day care costs range between $400 and $700 per month *per child.* Multiply that by two, three, or more and ...*OUCH!*

TIP!

Day care costs for multiples can very easily exceed the rent or mortgage payment and car payments combined!!

THE SEARCH

Once you have found a day care center that has multiple openings, take the time to visit and interview the staff. Compile a list of questions, make a copy for each center you visit, and take lots of notes. Use our questionnaire as a guide to collect the information with which you can make a sound decision. Hold on to your notes in case you have to go through the search process again.

THE FACILITY
Before Choosing a Day Care Center:

✖ Get recommendations.

✖ Make sure they are licensed and inspected.

✖ Drop in unannounced so you can see the facility in action, not at a prescribed time or naptime.

At the Day Care Center, Ask:

✖ How long have they been in business?

- What hours is the facility open?
- What is their policy for late pick-up?
- Is the staff trained in CPR and first aid?
- How much does it cost?
- Do they offer discounts for multiples?

THE CHILDREN'S WELL-BEING
Ask:

- Will they eat well?
- What happens when one or all of your children become sick?
- What it the ratio of infants and toddlers to caregivers?
- What is the general attitude of the caregivers and are they genuinely engaged with the children?
- Do they provide a caring and responsive environment?
- Does the environment foster development with age-appropriate toys, equipment, and activities?

QUESTIONS FOR YOU
Ask Yourself:

- Will they gain a greater attachment to the caregivers than to you, the parents?
- Can you handle the rigid logistics of drop-off and pick-up every workday?
- How does the cost compare to hiring in-home care?
- Where do you think the children will thrive best? At home or with more social contact?
- Will they constantly be exposed to colds and illness from other children?
- Can you afford it?

"They'll Probably Just Play with the Boxes Anyway"—Inexpensive Toys and Play

INEXPENSIVE PLAY IDEAS REQUIRE LESS IMAGINATION THAN YOU THINK!

Infants and toddlers are fascinated by what you and I might think are the simplest things. There's not a day that goes by when we're not on our hands and knees looking for the missing shoelaces to Bill's favorite pair of Rockports or picking up a mountain of facial tissue off the floor that one or all of them have pulled out one by one.

Relive your childhood with inexpensive ways to encourage and develop your children's skills while having loads of fun!

> "I went to our local newspaper and bought the end of a roll of paper. We roll it on the kitchen floor, and the children love to color on it."
>
> —SE, Roseburg, Ore.
> The Triplet Connection

> "I let my kids develop their own imaginations by letting them play with dirt, leaves, rocks, and bugs.... Tupperware and water are a lot of fun in the backyard. I let them play with the hose and let them water the yard... dogs... toys... each other."
>
> —GW, Fairfield, Calif.

DOLLAR STORES

Dollar stores are loaded with inexpensive toys that will occupy small children. They also have general household supplies for a fraction of what you would pay in a general retail store. For the shopaholics, dollar stores can also be a place to "get lost in" without putting a huge dent in the budget.

> "We bought a twelve-pack of multi-colored soft sponges for a buck at the dollar store, and before we got a chance to use them the kids discovered them and wouldn't give them back! They played with them all the time and we used them to teach colors."
>
> —All-for-a-Dollar Bill

LAUNDRY BASKETS

Pick them up at a dollar store for a buck! Laundry baskets can be a great source of fun for the babies.

- They fill them up with toys and empty them over and over again.

- They push them across the floor from one end of the room to the other.

- They put them over their heads and over yours and play peek-a-boo.

- They love to imitate you as they pretend to fold laundry with their baskets.

WATER

There are endless ways to play with water in the appropriate settings. Of course, never leave your children alone when playing with water.

- An old-time favorite is running through the sprinkler.

- Backyard wading pools loaded with cups, small pails, shovels, or anything that will pour water will keep your little ones busy for long stretches of time.

- Give them clean paint rollers and paint brushes, just like Daddy, to dip in the wading pool or a bucket of sudsy water and soon your little Rembrandts will be "painting" everything in sight with water.

- Save plastic sports water bottles and fill them with water for outdoor fun.

- Let them go wild with chalk on the sidewalk. Extend this spontaneous artistic expression to the next day by giving them clean paint brushes dipped in buckets of water to smear over their sidewalk chalk creations. The concrete canvases will keep them occupied for long stretches of time.

- Give them a sponge and let them help you wash the car.

No-Mess Finger Paints

> *"Put one quarter cup of starch and three tablespoons of powdered tempera paint in a large resealable plastic bag. Squeeze the air out of the bag, lock it, and then seal it tightly with a piece of masking tape. Squeeze the bag gently to blend the paint and starch. Put the bag flat on the table and use your fingers to create pictures. 'Erase' by smoothing out the bag."*
>
> —LV, Upper Sandusky, Ohio
> **The Triplet Connection**

Reading and Singing

Anyone who has tried it knows that reading to two or more at the same time, with four, six, or eight little hands all grasping at different pages simultaneously, doesn't work!

> *"Be creative. My kids love to hear me read or sing a song."*
> — KD, N. Olmstead, Ohio

❇ Reading usually works best one-on-one during the first three years.

❇ Books or songs on tape can be just as entertaining and will aid in language development. Kids love the repetition of hearing things over and over again!

> *"We sing and chant with the babies all the time. Their best cheer is 'D-A-D-D-Y!! Daddy! Daddy! He's Our Guy!'"*
> —Bill

> *"Reading was a hassle since all three wanted to sit on my lap at once. Now they each pick one or two books, and then they sit on my lap for 'their' book."*
>
> —CH, Jenison, Mich.
> **The Triplet Connection**

"Trying to read to all three at one time was not a rewarding experience until they were four years old. Before that time, I felt unable to respond to each child's needs, comments, follow their interests, etc.... If you only have the gumption to read to one child per day, do that. There is no rule that says every child has to get his or her turn the same day!"

—JG, Warrenville, Ohio
The Triplet Connection

Hide-and-Seek

What fun this game is with multiples!

Containers and Cartons

- Take a large plastic pretzel jar, the kind you find at SAM's Club, and cover it with any kind of paper. You can play "Discover What's Inside?" as they reach inside and pull out a toy.
- Do the same with an empty cereal box.
- Egg cartons make great places for the babies to stash their little treasures. They'll put stuff in and take stuff out of these jars, boxes, and cartons as all day long!
- Empty spice containers and plastic salt and pepper sellers are great in the sand box.

The Local Community

Local libraries offer toddlers' story hour and other children's events. The library also can provide information on local parks, recreation centers, zoos, children's museums, and community activities.

"McDonald's playland—fun and french fries!"
—TG, Warrenville, Ohio

TIP!

This is a time to relive the fun and games of your childhood. Remember, you are only limited by your imagination.

Chapter Seven

"Who Are All These Little People?"— The Second and Third Years

"The Terrible Twos Times... X"—Multiple Struggles for Autonomy

At first it's really hard, then it gets easier, then harder again. We prefer to call this period the "*Trouble Twos*" because there is nothing really terrible about children seeing and experiencing things for the first time in their lives. What makes it terrible is that even as they master their newly discovered skills, they haven't quite figured out when it's appropriate to use them! Your freewheeling toddlers will climb on tables and counters; drop spoons and bowls filled with food from the table; pour milk and shampoo on the carpet; pull electrical plugs, the dog's tail, each other's hair; push doors, drawers, and each other; and leave chaos in their wake. They get into trouble faster than you can say "*Oh, no!*" and will keep you busier than a one-armed wallpaper hanger. Approach this stage as a journey of wonderment and discovery. Stay flexible, drink plenty of coffee, and keep a sense of humor; you're going to need it!

"We Don't Climb on the Table"— Teaching Basic Social Skills and Manners

The key to teaching your children basic social skills and mannersis repetition and consistency. Catch the bad behavior immediately and correct the child. Tell him or her the rule about the couch, door, VCR, tabletop, or their brother's head, and don't make exceptions. Remember, if little Bobby is not allowed to use little Mary for broccoli target practice, Mary is not allowed to paint little Timmy's hair with pudding.

> *"The good news with multiples is you get to go through this once and for all and then you're done. The bad news is that they all go through it at the same time!"*
>
> —**Bill Going Bonkers**

At home, it may not matter that your children have decided that the best place to watch TV is standing on the table. But at your new neighbor's house—you know, the one with the expensive glass sculptured coffee table—the same viewing experience may not be appreciated. To children a table is a table. If it's OK to stand on one, it's OK to stand on them all.

> **TIP!**
>
> **Teach them to behave at home as you would like them to behave in public.**
>
> **Begin teaching them good behavior and manners early. The work required now will pale in comparison to what you would otherwise face in the future.**

Make good manners and social skills part of the basics. As they learn new words like "milk," "juice," and "cookie" make "please" and "thank you" part of the process required to get the result they want. Every time! Remember, you have to set a good example yourself. Children watch and imitate. They like to do what you do. So you will have to clean up your act as well. Finally, remember to acknowledge appropriate behavior. If it's fun, they will want to do it again.

> *"Always, from one year old, talk to them the way you want them to talk to you and others; please, thank you, excuse me. One year old is not too young—then it becomes habit."*
>
> —BT, N. Olmstead, Ohio

"OK, Who Started It?"— Discipline for One and for All

When your babies approach the age of eighteen to twenty-four months, you might as well get yourselves a couple of black and white striped referee shirts and a whistle because refereeing is going to be your job for the next year.

Two three, four, or more are a stronger force than one, and this contributes to all the mischief they get into.

> **TIP!**
>
> **It will take the wisdom of Solomon and the patience of Job to deal with the conflicts between them and to defend yourself against their joint capers and conspiracies.**

Like all children, multiples are curious and are constantly exploring the boundaries of their world. Unlike singletons, however, their explorations enjoy the added dimension of group dynamics. Each new trick is greeted with encouragement and immediate emulation.

> *"I swear, there are times when they all look at each other, and in the same moment, dump their bowls upside down and wear them as hats on top of their heads. Other times, one will start blowing bubbles with Jell-O and the others immediately join in."*
>
> —Sheila, with Wonder

Together, multiples:

1. Learn to take their clothes off at the same time.

2. Learn to unplug everything and present you with handfuls of plastic outlet covers.

3. Learn to pull the sheets off their mattresses, cry for them to be put back on, only to remove them again and again.

4. Pull each other's socks and shoes off just after you have put them on for the third time.

5. Learn to open and pour anything and everything that comes in a box or sippy cup onto the floor.

6. Learn to bite each other when they play or get mad.

7. Discover how to turn their playhouse upside down and climb on top of it to reach the cabinet with the shiny crystal.

8. Use each other to climb up onto the kitchen counter tops.

9. Throw their cups to the floor in sequence as if training for the Rockettes in New York.

10. Learn to stash their personal supply of animal crackers into the VCR.

11. Use anything they can lift as a hammer.

12. Use anything they can reach as a nail, including their siblings.

"There will be gum and other assorted objects in their hair and bumps on their heads, because siblings always wonder what it sounds like to bounce objects off their noggins."

—Kyle and Crew, Ariz.

Double Trouble and Triple Time-Outs

Unacceptable behavior such as biting, hitting, and fighting among them is inevitable. Children at this age can understand rules. However you choose to discipline your children, remember one thing, be consistent.

Use time-outs and make them say "I'm sorry" to the other person.

❖ Put up a gate separating the hallway from the main area. If the child doesn't respond to a warning, put the child in the penned area for a minute or two.

❖ If you don't like the penalty box method, try a cool-off zone. Ahead of time, have your child help you create a comfortable cool-off area with soft blankets, animals, or books. When their behavior gets out of line, tell them to "cool off" and return only when they are feeling better.

> *"When two of ours are fighting over a toy, my wife often threatens, 'Am I going to have to put that toy on a time-out?' The problem usually resolves itself."*
>
> —ST, Father of Triplets, Calif.

When things have settled down, reintroduce the toy and reinforce the concepts of sharing and taking turns.

"In your spare time," check out the book *Time-Out For Toddlers* by Dr. James W. Varni and Donna G. Corwin. It is filled with terrific information and positive tactics to effectively deal with normal childhood misbehavior for ages two to six years.

"Double the Bubbles"— Making Bath Time Efficient and Fun

During the first six months it is OK to bathe them once every two to three days, with a little sponge bath in between as necessary. During this time, carefully bathe them separately.

ASSEMBLY-LINE STYLE!

Although it can be done alone, bathing all your babies works best with a team to insure supervision and safety. Set everything up in advance: shampoo, soap, towels, powder, diapers, etc. Bathe one baby at a time, and hand the clean wet one off to your partner to dry, powder, diaper, and clothe.

We have had success bathing one baby at a time in the shower. Have your partner hand one baby to you while in the shower. Do a quick lather and rinse and add a few warm snuggles and then hand the baby off to your partner. This does not really save any time but it is fun. **Be careful! Use extra caution because the babies are very slippery!**

GOING SOLO

If bathing them by yourself, bathe one baby at a time and keep the others nearby so that you can keep a close watch on them. When they are older, bathe one baby and keep the others corralled in a safe area. We were successful in closing the bathroom door while leaving the others in a secured baby-proofed area such as the hallway or the nursery. Wherever it is, be sure it is a place you can feel assured that they can not get into trouble if left alone for a few minutes while you bathe one of them.

"This way they stay out of your hair, out of the toilet paper, and out of the bathroom drawers, and you can concentrate on the baby in the tub."
—Bill and the Bubbles

You can leave them to roam the bathroom with you and the other baby, but we found that there is too much temptation to get into stuff, regardless of how well you have baby-proofed. Plus, as they get older they try to climb into the tub, creating chaos for everyone.

Old-fashioned Bath Time Fun!

We've burned through enough reams of videotape from bath time to blanket. Put them all in together and get ready for a splash party! The babies love the water and it relaxes them. You get a break too as you can sit and enjoy them as you keep a watch and ensure their safety.

Here are a few more bath tips:

"Let them play with squirt sports bottles, and anything plastic that they can pour water from, including shovels and pails. You sit back and enjoy. Keep the camera nearby!"

—Sheila

* Even though you may have a tub full of wet kids and toys, bath time can be an opportunity to provide special one-on-one attention if you have another adult to supervise the others. Talking and singing with the child can be very relaxing and rewarding for both of you.

* It's a good idea to use non-slip bath mats and soft plastic faucet covers. They'll cut down on unnecessary slips and bumps on the head.

"Once the babies stopped using their infant crib mirror in their beds any longer, we attached it to the tile soap dish holder in the bathtub with suction cups. They love using it there. It occupies two while I bathe the third."

—KF, Park Forest, Ill.
The Triplet Connection

* It's a good idea to set your hot water heater down to 120 degrees Fahrenheit so that if a baby happens to reach over and turn on the hot water before you can grab them, they won't get burned. Scald burns in little kids are all too common for that very reason.

TIP! **Use bath time as an opportunity to cut down on clean-up.**

"Popsicles in the tub at bath time."
—GW, Fairfield, Calif.

"When required, we give them their syrupy medicine in the bathtub. They love it, and all the sticky drips go right down the drain."
—Bill and the Bunch

"When my boys were one to two years old, I'd give them a bath and spoon feed them all at the same time. They played and entertained each other while they ate and got clean. The mess goes right down the drain!"
—CB, Salisbury, NC
The Triplet Connection

"To make bath time easier, a hand held shower massager can let you give them a quick shower, and a shampoo shield, found in mail order catalogs, makes shampoos a snap."
—ST, Charlottesville, Va.
The Triplet Connection

"Let them learn to drink from a real cup while sitting in the tub."
—BB, Canton, Ohio

"Visitors in the Night"—
The Transition from Cribs to Beds

Making the transition is inevitable. Somewhere between eighteen months and three years, or whenever they climb, fly, or fall out of their cribs—whichever comes first—is the time to make the transition. But the question is, how do you do it when there are more than one?

We've heard everything from horror stories of toddlers flipping their mattresses onto the headboards and climbing them like ladders, and couples cutting the bedroom doors in half so that they could look in on the children at any time without being rushed at by three little critters when opening the door, to transitions that were made easy thanks to sleeping bags and pup tents.

"When my son climbed out and fell hard to the floor (it was a surprise—I didn't think they could do it yet) it was a big enough scare that I got rid of the cribs and put in beds immediately."

—DB, Puxico, Mo.

"They started climbing out at two. We put crib mattresses on the floor for six months then bought big beds."

—JB, Birmingham, Ala.

"It was NOT an easy transition. They were gone for a weekend visit with their father and when they came back, they had new beds, which they thought were very exciting. Getting them to stay in bed and go to sleep was very rough, but I would have rather dealt with that than a trip to the ER from a fall from the crib."

—DB, Puxico, Mo.

"We bought toddler beds because of the lack of space and asked Santa to bring them when our triplets were two. They were so excited about the beds that we never had difficulty getting them comfortable. Bedtime at night was no problem, but prepare yourself for a difficult stage with naps."

—SN, New Philadelphia, Ohio

Some tips for the transition to a "big kid bed":

�֍ A good approach is to put twin mattresses on the floor, and then introduce the twin bed frame with a soft safety rail.

✖ A good technique for when they transition into toddler beds is to keep their bedroom door open, put up a gate, and park yourself outside with a magazine, just out of their sight. When you hear your little army starting to climb out of bed, give them their "orders." You'll spend less time running back and forth.

✖ A fixed bedtime routine lets the children know what to expect every night.

✖ Use bedtime rituals such as a bath, a story, or a prayer.

✖ Be firm. Give them a warning and shut the door. Their fussing will be short-lived and they will soon drop off to sleep—if you're lucky.

"Look What I Did!"—Potty Training Made Easy (Well, Almost)

With two, three, four, or more doing it all at once, plan on spending a lot of time in the bathroom. There are some general guidelines that have been consistent with all the parents we have talked with.

> "I spent the entire summer in the bathroom with my triplets, but then it was done."
>
> —PW, Lydhurst, Ohio

WAIT

Don't push your children or expect them to be ready at a certain age just because one of the others is. Boys, for instance, usually aren't ready as early as girls. If you wait until you are sure they're ready, it will happen practically overnight. Most parents of multiples have told us that their kids weren't ready until they were two and a half to three years old. Remember, they are all individuals and it is possible they may potty train one year apart.

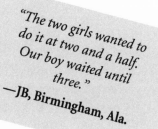

"The two girls wanted to do it at two and a half. Our boy waited until three."

—JB, Birmingham, Ala.

"I always waited until they said they were ready. They all learned by three, and it took less than a week."

—GW, Fairfield, Calif.

MAKE IT POTTY PARTY TIME

- ✖ If it's fun, they'll look forward to doing it. Make it fun.

- ✖ Reward them for all their little accomplishments. Telling you, using the toilet, wiping, and flushing are all reasons to celebrate.

- ✖ Don't punish for accidents; they happen.

- ✖ Use an accident as a teaching opportunity.

- ✖ React swiftly and don't keep a wet or soiled diaper on for long. It may be confusing for someone who only has a learner's permit.

> *"They all love to wear 'big girl' panties or 'big boy' pants."*
>
> —JB, Birmingham, Ala.

> *"It was a competitive game between the three of them and it worked!"*
>
> —BT, N. Olmstead, Ohio

SPEED

Their little bodies won't give you much time. Don't be surprised if you find yourself frantically racing around looking for the nearest toilet as fast as you can on your next outing. When little Jimmy has got to go, he means NOW!

> "Toilet training was quickly mastered. First, we didn't even try to begin until age two and a half. They used three potty seats, special 'Barbie' panties, and M&M's as a reward. The entire process took about three weeks."
>
> —KP, Bayshore, NY
> The Triplet Connection

> "We waited until two and three-quarter years. It was easy!! We made them go every half hour. If they went, even a little, they got one or two M&M's. They were trained totally in less than two weeks."
>
> —JB, University Heights, Ohio

READY, AIM, FIRE!

Many parents have used the Cheerio or Fruit Loop approach. Drop a few of pieces of cereal in the toilet bowl and see if the children can hit the target! Reward them with a tiny treat if the mission is successful.

 TIP!

Don't dress them in overalls while potty training! Have girls wear dresses.

Wait until they're ready regardless of how old they are or whose two-year-old kid has already been trained. Good luck!

Chapter Eight

"The Instant Family Doesn't Come with Instructions" Making It Work and Building Quality Relationships

Children Are Like Snowflakes... Recognizing Their Individuality

Whether the babies are identical, fraternal, or a combination thereof, recognizing their individuality is critical to their self-esteem and positive development. Multiples receive a lot of attention just for being multiples. The only thing they share in common is their birthday, and that's where it ends.

❖ Being ooo'd over and being referred to as a unit does not help to build self-esteem.

❖ Referring to them by their names, and not as "the twins," "the triplets," "the quads," will help to foster their uniqueness. This includes introducing them by name, openly referring to them by name, and gently encouraging others to do the same. You can establish this very early on, and the sooner the better.

TIP!
The children will have their fill of being lumped together as they go out in public and off to school.

Be aware that even though you may have asked friends and family to refer to them as individuals, you cannot count on them to always comply with your wishes. It is easier to cluster than it is to differentiate, and people enjoy the opportunity to express their "bragging rights" as the aunt or uncle of twins or triplets, so parents should take the lead on this issue and recognize the children individually for who they are and set good examples for others to follow.

TIP!
You will find that the terms "twins," "triplets," and "quads" are used by people outside the family. Around home they are just "the babies."

DRESSING THEM ALIKE OR NOT

For some parents, dressing their children in those adorable matching outfits gives them much pleasure as they proudly present their children to the world as multiples. They love the "double takes" from strangers and welcome the opportunity to tell everyone who asks about their children. Other parents deliberately dress them differently, so that they will be regarded as individuals and not as a unit. Regardless of what parents feel about society's perception of who they are, or the effect it will have on the children's perception of themselves, one thing is for sure:

TIP!
Most parents of multiples tell us they dress them in whatever is clean that day!

Individual Photo Albums

Create a photo album for each child with pictures of just themselves. Keep the group shots in a separate family photo album.

Baby's First Calendar

Hallmark makes a *Baby's First Calendar* kit, complete with a stock of stickers to mark their first smiles and rollovers, first tooth, first step, and other baby firsts. Buy one for each child, and write special notes on them when the babies do something new. Keep them in an accessible and fixed place, such as the nursery or kitchen, so you can get to them when a special moments happens.

Make your own calendars by taking regular calendars and personalizing them with a picture of each baby on each calendar.

Baby Scrapbooks

Make individual scrapbooks to keep all of their special items: such as birth announcements, first haircut clippings, ultrasound images. If you are too busy to organize this, put all of the items together in one place, and divide the stash by each child. Then complete them when they are older and you have more time.

> *"Keep the scrapbooks where you spend most of your time so you don't forget a special moment or date."*
>
> — KD, N. Olmstead, Ohio

Baby Time Capsules

Create time capsules for each baby. They can be as simple as boxes or large popcorn tins. Fill each one with interesting items that represent the era in which they were born: current events of the day, fads, fashion trends, and even the price of a gallon of milk.

❖ Have your family save extra copies of the newspaper on the day your babies are born.

❖ Include *Life Magazine's* issue "The Year In Pictures."

We included the babies' first bottles from the hospital that measured their intake by cc's—representative of their tiny tummies! This will be enjoyed in years to come as you look back and see how the world has changed.

"The Bombay Company makes a beautiful wooden hinged 'Memory Box' with a brass inscribed nameplate perfect to hold their individual birth announcements, and other special mementos and baby keepsakes."

—BS, Highland Heights, Ohio

Possessions

Multiples experience more than their fair share of sharing, but not everything has to be shared. Let each one have their own special items—little things like their own special bibs or a set of pajamas. Everyone, including each child, is entitled to ownership of certain things.

"We worked on establishing ownership for certain critical items, and one key trick for us was color-coding or initialing some toys. We started the color-coding when they were babies, and then used letters when they learned the first initial of their names. This really worked for us in cutting down on the fighting… and not EVERYTHING has to be shared! It seems pretty clear to everyone what belongs to whom, and they pretty much respect each other's property."

—LL, Morrow, Ohio

More Ways to Acknowledge Their Individuality

- Decorate each of their cribs differently. Use different stuffed animals, mix up the patterns in the sheets, blankets, and accessories. You can still have the same themes or color schemes throughout the nursery, but pay attention to respecting the babies as individual people.

- When they are a little older, go shopping together and let them take turns picking out the "treats." Just because one likes something doesn't mean it's the others' favorite too.
- Don't forget to praise your children for who they are. So often children are praised for what they DO in an effort to reinforce good behavior. Praising them for their good personal qualities and attributes helps them to realize their uniqueness.

"When our triplets were two, I bought them a Little Mermaid calendar. Each day of the month is designated as someone's day. I go in order, first Monica, second Nicholas, third Christopher, fourth Monica.... On 'their day' they get to pick the video for the day, or the stories. It's a great tie-breaker and keeps the parents from being the bad guys. It also prevents one from dominating the group. We've been doing this for a year now and when they want to watch a video they run to the calendar and say 'whose day is it Mommy?'"

—C and F, Solon, Ohio

TIP!

If you're one to tell your baby girl(s) that she/they are so beautiful, don't forget to add *"and so smart!"* Your positive encouragement can go a long way in helping her succeed.

"Look at Me!"—One-On-One Time

Young toddlers seem to learn best when they interact one-on-one with you, and do not respond well, if at all, to group activities. So why is it that they want to be involved in whatever activity you are engaged in with the other child?

TIP!

Any parent of multiple toddlers knows you can't read a book to two, three, or more of them at the same time, yet they will insist! It is no different than when one has a boo-boo—they all have (imaginary) boo-boos.

The children are individuals, with different personalities and different needs for attention. One might be shy, another very independent, while another puts new meaning in the term "Mama's Boy." The reality is that it is impossible to divide your time equally between them. Some children will be more aggressive in gaining your attention as they pull and tug on you, while others may be less demonstrative and less vocal, but equally in need of your undivided attention. It is easy for the less assertive child to get lost in the shuffle. Recognizing the children's individual needs for attention, and making the time to address them, will foster confidence and self-esteem.

By spending one-on-one time with each child, you can help your children grow individually, while still respecting the unique bond that is inherent to multiples. Spending time alone with one child allows you to really focus on them individually. There is no interference, fighting, or competition, and with one child at a time it is soooo much easier.

ONE-ON-ONE TIME DOESN'T HAVE TO COST MONEY!

If one-on-one time means spending money you don't have, or if it creates logistical challenges for the family, try something simple. Let ordinary time become special time:

❖ Fold laundry together. Or should we say, *unfold* laundry together. It's best to give them their own pile since they just play with it and run off with bits and pieces of it.

❖ Have one-on-one talks with one child each day. As with reading, there is no law that says you must spend equal time every day with each child to talk, read, or whatever. Make a conscious effort to balance these activities over the course of a week.

- Take a bath with just one baby.

- Give special piggy-back rides.

- When running errands, take one child while leaving the others with your partner. Use this time to talk, play, sing, or whatever else to turn them into one-on-one adventures.

> "Hire a sitter one morning a week and take one child out to breakfast and grocery shopping. Let him or her select cereal and snacks for the family."
>
> —BL, Chagrin Falls, Ohio

- Let family members, including grandparents and other parents, know that it is OK to invite only one of the multiples over, and that they can play apart. This can become an excellent opportunity for you and your partner to spend special time with the remaining children.

- Support individual interests, and encourage them to make their own choices. When serving ice cream, for example, while everyone gets vanilla, let him or her pick the color of their cone.

> "A good time and place for one-on-one time is on the changing table or in their high chairs. They are captives and attentive. They are also in a good position to play 'where are your toes?' 'where is your nose?' One thing you may want to avoid while eating is 'where is your hair?'"
>
> —Bill and the Babies

- Take the opportunity, when engaged in routine tasks like washing hands and tying shoes, to have a special moment with each of the children. Talk to them personally, practice words, give them an extra hug and tell them how much you love them.

- Schedule a specific time for each child to have one-on-one time. Ask them what they would like to do. Older toddlers can look forward to their special time, and since every child gets their own scheduled time, this helps to introduce the concept of taking turns.

With multiples, individual attention can run thin. We often wondered what adverse affects might be in the making because we didn't have the opportunity to concentrate on one baby. Here are some thoughts to soothe your soul:

> *"We scheduled days—one for each child and one for Mom!"*
> **—BT, N. Olmstead, Ohio**

- Babies sometimes need their own space. Consider what happens when a baby is overstimulated by people, places, noises—it's likely to result in a disaster. They too need private time. It is hard to sit with each child and read to them individually, and teach them new words. I thought that by not interacting with them individually as much as I wanted to, they would be bored and under-stimulated. But it's OK to leave it up to your babies to occupy themselves. Let them control the interactions with you; they will let you know when they want your participation. Keep in mind that they have each other to interact with.

"Multiples Make Great Team Players"—Learning to Share and Take Turns

Multiples tend to grasp the concepts of sharing and compromise early on. They experience conflicts and battles over toys and other worldly possessions among themselves. It can sound like the final seconds of a tied basketball game at home court as they all desperately chime in with "their case" for the toy!

With your guidance, they can learn early on to compromise or just go get another toy. When they are fighting over a toy, sit down with them and supervise, sharing and taking turns until all but one loses interest. You can provide guidance during the battles by addressing the child's needs and feelings, while at the same time acknowledging the needs and feelings of the other siblings involved.

Early exposure to conflict management skills can lead to a greater willingness to share and compromise. With your guidance, they learn how to resolve their own disputes amicably and independently. As they develop this valuable skill they will soon find creative ways to resolve their own battles, and you get to stay out of it!

- You have to pick your battles, too. There are times when it is appropriate for you to just stay out of it, otherwise they will come running to you to resolve every little conflict that arises.
- If possible, buy identical toys for each child.
- When the children "melt-down," call it a day.
- Consider yourself lucky, they have their own built-in playmates and their interests will be on the same developmental level.

"To me, this is a big part of being a triplet. They always have to share and they seem to learn this faster and better than their singleton counterparts."

—JB, University Heights, Ohio

"When they fight over the toy, gently take one child aside and ask him or her to find the other identical toy. Try to make the hunt fun!"

—Bill and the Bunch

"Constantly saying 'please' and 'thank you'; and whenever they fight, I say 'share'– now they say these words to each other!"

KD, N. Olmstead, Ohio

"One way to teach sharing is to fill one sippy cup with their favorite juice and play the sharing game. Give the cup to one child, count out loud to five, and then give it to the next child while explaining it is now his or her turn. You'll be surprised at how fast they catch on."

—Bill

> *"If the kids are fighting over a particular toy, I let them.*
> *They soon settle their own disputes without any*
> *choosing or favoritism on my part, and it seems to make*
> *them want to share more. They tend to give things up*
> *more easily than single children I've seen."*
>
> —CD, Peculiar, Mo.
> **The Triplet Connection**

"One Is the Loneliest Number"— Older and Younger Sibling Adjustment

Sibling rivalry is difficult enough, but when a sibling must compete with multiples for attention, it can seem overwhelming. An older child may express jealousy, aggression, sadness, or rebellion. With so much going on and so many demands on your time, it is easy to miss the signals that your older child is giving you. That is why it is so important to make time for your singleton child.

The arrival of multiples is a major event for the entire family. For the older sibling(s) it will be an upheaval, as the parents begin to ration time that was once devoted entirely to the older child. The adjustment will come easier for some than others, and here are some ideas to help make the transition a little smoother and hopefully minimize the acting out.

- Introduce the new babies as soon as you can—in pregnancy.
- Ask the child to bring a gift—a drawing or a stuffed animal perhaps, and have a gift to give from the babies.
- Encourage and help the child express his or her feelings.

KEEP THEM INCLUDED

Remind friends and visitors gently that the twins or triplets are not your only children and ask them to say hello to your other children. Let older siblings participate in the feeding and nurturing.

"I always introduce the older sibling first. 'This is my best friend and son...'"

—BT, N. Olmstead, Ohio

"We always mention and include our older child (a girl twenty-two months older). She is very well adjusted and is not threatened by the triplets."

—JB, Birmingham, Ala.

MAKE TIME FOR THEM

Set aside time on the calendar for quality time with the older sibling. Make a permanent arrangement with a sitter and get out of the house. Go to dinner or the movies, go shopping, or do a favorite activity together. They need time away from the babies, too.

Use the babies' naptime to cuddle up and read together or do other favorite one-on-one activities.

"My eleven-year-old son adjusted well. I always feel guilty though, that I don't have the time for him that I had before. I think he's a little relieved though, he says I was smothering him."

—TG, Mentor, Ohio

"We take car rides (the four kids and Mom). The babies are quiet, and I can have a good long conversation with my eleven-year-old son!"

—TG, Mentor, Ohio

"I have a daughter almost exactly three years younger than the triplets. My biggest concern before she was born was that they wouldn't want to share Mommy. I shouldn't have worried, as they think she is just wonderful. The most difficult part, for me, is not always being able to do things with the older three because the younger one can't participate and nobody else is available to watch her."

—DB, Puxico, Mo.

"We're All in This Together"

Believe it or not, by eighteen months the babies can start to put things away. Although this may sometimes mean putting shoes inside drawers and heaps of toys in the microwave, by eighteen months they are at least demonstrating their desire to perform tasks by themselves. You can capitalize on their eagerness and make clean-up tasks a fun game they will want to participate in.

❈ Teach them early to push their chairs under the table.

❈ Challenge them to sort toys by color—a separate bin for each color.

❈ Starting when they are around three years old, play clean-up games using music or play "race against the clock."

❈ Try singing and chanting to make cleaning tasks fun!

❈ Send them on a shoe hunt to make a game out of rounding up shoes.

❈ As they get older, send them on missions. Have one fetch a diaper or towel for you and give an extra hug and words of encouragement when they deliver. These little tasks will help you out, make them feel special, and build self-esteem.

❈ Do it again and again. Repetition and practice are the keys to learning.

❈ Tell them *thank you.* This helps the children understand that their contribution was appreciated and helps to reinforce cooperative behavior.

> "As soon as they can be independent—let them! They can dress themselves, pick up their room, toys, etc. at an early age."
>
> —JB, University Heights, Ohio

❈ Once again, laundry baskets or the plastic milk-crate style bins available at office supply stores come to the rescue! Rather than dumping all toys into a central toy chest, designate separate baskets, crates, or bins for books, toy cars and trucks, balls, dolls, etc. This keeps the clutter down and helps teach the children basic organization skills.

STRESS BUSTERS

In one word, stress. Mentally, physically, and psychologically, raising multiples is draining. We cannot eliminate the stress the babies bring, but we can manage it.

"The stress kicks in at about six months."
—Maureen Doolan Boyle, Founder, MOST

"Take one day at a time and keep a sense of humor. If one person becomes frustrated, let someone else take over."

—JJ, Bradenton, Fla.
The Triplet Connection

"Work out. Make sure you get time for yourself even if it means hiring two babysitters."
—JB, Universtiy Heights, Ohio

"Laugh, get away sometimes, exercise."

—JB, Birmingham, Ala.

More stress busters:

- Give yourself lots of time-outs .
- Remind yourself, "this is only a stage and it too will pass."
- Never underestimate yourself and your ability to deal with what life hands you.
- When you say "I can't"—say "*yes, I can.*"
- Minimize your external stress factors. For example, keep your to-do list short.
- Take a deep breath, load 'em up, and get out of the house. A quick errand, a stroll in the mall, or simply a walk in the fresh air can have a lifting effect.
- Hire a sitter after the babies are down for the night, and get out of the house. If you are too tired to take a walk, sit on the porch.

✷ If the babies sleep well in the van, consider going for a Sunday afternoon drive on a Tuesday morning. This will get you out of the house, break up the routine, and help you to reconnect with the rest of the world while they sleep.

✷ Take one day at a time.

✷ Multiples require a great deal of patience on the parents' part. When the stress seems too much, find something like a poem or prayer that will help you regain your patience and perspective.

✷ Always know where your keys are. Designate one location for your house and car keys and never deviate. Have a back-up set made just in case and keep them somewhere special.

> *"Don't give up! I take care of my children alone, calling on help when I reach my limit or need a break. When I can't find the help I need, I call on God, who gives me the strength."*
>
> **—PA, Apo, N.Y.**
> **The Triplet Connection**

Avoiding Tailspins and Meltdowns

Taking a deep breath and staying cool is the best tactic. Your babies pick up your stress vibes and anxieties more than you might know. When they are stressed and you are stressed, the results can be a disaster. Calmness breeds calmness. When you remain calm, the upset baby feels reassured and will calm down in turn, sooner rather than later. Try to stay calm. They react to your emotions, your body language, the tension and volume in your voice, and even the way you hold them.

> *"I try to tackle the smaller problems quickly to reduce the number of things hanging over my head. There are times, too, when I simply give up and cry, and then get started again. Other days I just do my best to 'forget' everything that needs to get done and spend the whole day just spending time with my kids."*
>
> **—DB, Puxico, Mo.**

Babies need their own space too, sometimes. One of the advantages of multiples is that they have each other to play and interact with, lessening the need for you to entertain them and keep them occupied. More importantly, this gives them the opportunity to set the pace of stimulation. Some singleton parents unknowingly overstimulate their babies in the pursuit of keeping them entertained. With multiples, it is easy to let your babies control their own level of stimulation and their interactions with you and each other. It's easier on the babies and easier on you. When they are ready for you to join in their play, they will let you know you.

"Deep breathing and my favorite CD—Autumn in New England."
—SN, New Philadelphia, Ohio

"Take three deep breaths and walk out of the room for five minutes... you'll feel better when you return."
—KD, N. Olmstead, Ohio

"Meet Me in the Laundry Room"— Finding Time for Each Other

Multiples will test you in many ways, and your marriage is not immune. Parents of multiples agree that the babies are the true test of the strength of their marriage, and most agree that the first year is the most difficult.

> *"The first year was the most difficult year in our lives: a true test of the strength of our marriage. Even though we had paid help and help from family and friends, we still lived in a state of exhaustion. I found myself snapping at my husband, not because of what he was or was not doing, but because I was so tired and frustrated from trying to keep everyone fed, changed, and happy."*
>
> **—Mother of Quadruplets, Decatur, Mo.**

Especially during that first year, caring for the babies requires both parents to sacrifice much of their personal freedom. The high costs of raising multiples can place a financial strain on the family and most couples prefer sleep over romance.

Just when the need for support and mutual understanding is the greatest, there is an inevitable change in the couple's relationship that can be especially difficult for first-time parents. This change involves a not-so-subtle shift toward regarding each other more as mother and father and less as husband and wife. What little time there is for talking with each other is often spent exchanging updates and reports on the babies. Conversations shift from exchanges of intimacy and support to, "Are these clean or dirty?" "Did you remember to put the baby blankets in the dryer?" "Have you seen her other shoe?" "Has he been changed yet?"

All of these factors can cause some couples to exhibit emotional distance and withdrawal. Others may experience resentment and anger. Deeper marital problems may require more than a kiss and a hug to make up. In some cases, the experience of raising multiples forces couples to look hard at what was an unstable relationship to begin with and get counseling to build or restore their relationship.

Contrary to popular belief, a survey conducted by MOST shows that most marriages of parents of multiples do not come apart at the seams.* Research among their membership, (on an average, 87 percent triplets, 11 percent quads, 2 percent quints) indicates that the divorce rate among multiple birth parents is actually much lower than in other marriages.

The national divorce rate is 50 percent. For marriages involving multiples: 99.9 percent were married at the time of conception, 98 percent are currently married, 1 percent divorced, .5 percent were widowed, and .5 percent never married.

It is important to recognize that although marriages involving multiple birth children may not end in divorce, they are not without their problems.

Thirty-five and a half percent of those surveyed felt they had experienced a significant amount of difficulty or stress, and 37 percent of them sought counseling. Forty-two percent of those who

---

*MOST Inc., Annual Research and Survey Results, 1987–1994.

experienced difficulty felt that it peaked during the first year after birth, 14 percent during the second and third years.

So, what can you do to make sure the relationship between you and your partner remains strong in the face of all the stress? Acknowledge the difficulties, show appreciation for each other's efforts, make time for each other, and keep the lines of communication open.

"Yes it's tough, at times unbearable... we would yell and sometimes scream at each other at the drop of a hat (always away from the kids). The first two years are very tough, and it will test all your patience and endurance. Just remember, it does get better as they get older. I feel that our experiences have strengthened me and my relationship with my wife."

—ST, Father of Triplets

"We don't have time to fight."

—SN, New Philadelphia, Ohio

"Recognize that you are both under stress and try to redirect your frustration away from each other in a healthy way. Go beat on a pillow until you feel better. This is when you need each other most."

—KR, Wadsworth, Ohio

"We have literally stepped out for a few stolen moments in the laundry room together. The background noise of the washer and dryer gave us a sense of temporary privacy and a chance to talk. This is a very tough job and we are not afraid to say so. Simply acknowledging and expressing your appreciation for the efforts of your partner can go a long way."

—Sheila and Bill

A few more tips:

✖ Make time for each other. Make an appointment and put a date on the calendar, and make a permanent arrangement with a sitter on those days. Pretend you are on a date, a romantic one. Focus your conversations on each other and not on a rerun of the day.

> *"I didn't think it would last. You are at each others' throats! This is where time together and time separate from each other helps a lot."*
>
> —KD, N. Olmstead, Ohio

✖ Turn off the TV.

✖ Turn off the computer.

✖ Turn the lights off. Have a candlelight dinner even if it's over frozen pizza.

✖ Keep talking to each other.

✖ Put a love-note somewhere where your partner is sure to find it.

> *"Communication is key. Make sure your spouse is your number one priority. Kids come second. It won't do your children any good if you have a poor marriage. Kids learn how to become parents by watching their own parents. Stay involved with a church for moral support. Go away on vacation at least once a year without your children. Renew your marriage and make time for each other."*
>
> —GW, Fairfield, Calif.

An Inexpensive Night Out!

Set up a babysitting exchange with other parents of multiples. After all, who could be more sympathetic to your situation?

> *"To get time alone as a couple, we have set up a babysitting exchange. We have become friends with a family who has twins. Since we both have multiples, we have a greater appreciation for the difficulty of having time alone. So we alternate Monday nights. On our night out, the husband stays at home with his own children, and the wife comes to stay with ours. The next week, we switch and they go out. This way the children are able to go to sleep in their own beds, and we get out for a couple of hours every other week with no money involved. We really look forward to this!"*
>
> —KJ, Yorba Linda, Calif.
> The Triplet Connection

"Time Off for Good Behavior"— Finding Time for Yourself

As caregivers of multiples, there is very little time left over at the end of the day for yourself. You will be burning the candle at both ends, and your needs are easily and often overlooked. They take a back seat to the needs of the babies and the wear and tear will catch up to you.

> *"One of my biggest fears was of becoming so buried in the babies' multiple needs that I would no longer be the spontaneous and happy person that I used to be."*
>
> —Confessions of a Triplet Mother

Carve Out a Slice of Time

Make arrangements to "step out of the ring" and make time for yourself. Get up a half-hour earlier and savor your morning coffee.

"I make it a priority to take time out for myself. If I feel like running away, I tell my spouse or get a sitter and just take off... even just to mindlessly shop for an hour. You will be happier, refreshed, and better able to handle the kids. Is it better to be there twenty-four hours a day stressed and yelling or to take off for a few hours and then appreciate the kids more when you are with them? I work part-time to help pay for a sitter. It doesn't matter if all my money goes to the sitter if I can get alone time."

—GW, Fairfield, Calif.

PUT IT ON THE CALENDAR IN INK

Plan two separate nights out per month for each spouse. Go out to dinner with a friend, the guys, the girls; go shopping, or go to a Starbucks and people-watch. Get out of the house.

Here are some inexpensive ways to enjoy some "alone time":

"Just like making a schedule, you just do it! This also gives the kids time with a different parent—remember, they get tired of you, too!"

—KD, N. Olmstead, Ohio

✖ Give yourself a good twenty to thirty minutes before bed to read a book or favorite magazine.

✖ Put on make-up or get your hair done.

✖ Get lost in Home Depot.

✖ Go the club and work out.

✖ Work on your car.

✖ Tinker on the Web.

"I have a sixty-minute drive to my office. This sixty-minute 'windshield time' is the thin slice of the day when I am not immersed in babies or business. Sometimes I crank up the CD player and pretend I'm Tina Turner, or call my sister to catch up on things. Other times I do nothing, and as I pull into the parking lot at the end of my hour, I ask myself, 'who drove?' Great therapy."

—Sheila Unwinds

"In the Doghouse"—Including the Family Pet

Even the beloved family pet will feel the impact of the "instant family." Little Fido may feel like he's being left out, so spend some extra time with him when you can. The bonus is that pets can be great stress-relievers for every member of the family. The unconditional love they display can be a real ego boost and they almost never reveal anything you tell them in confidence. With proper training (for both the pet and the children) they can also provide a pleasant diversion for the babies.

"When our babies came home, our dog, Buddy, didn't like his new ranking. He demonstrated this to us when he looked us straight in the eye and hiked his leg right in the middle of the room.... Now when the babies go out for an outing with out him, Buddy cries for them."

—Sheila and Bill in the Doghouse

Some tips to ensure harmony between the babies and your pets:

- Introduce the babies to your pets before they come home, by bringing a piece of the babies' clothing from the hospital in a plastic bag for your animals to sniff and become familiar with.
- Introduce the babies in person, and repeatedly say "nice baby… good Fido…." When Fido goes near the babies for a sniff, do the same, "nice baby… nice Fido."

❖ When the kisses and hugs get passed around make sure you include the family pet.

❖ As the babies get older, teach them to interact with the family pet by softly stroking their hands on the pet's coat and saying, "nice puppy," "nice kitty," or "gentle… gentle."

"Our dog runs and hides. Just don't forget he's there, especially if he was there before the kids. Give special attention to the dog when the kids are sleeping."

—KD, N. Olmstead, Ohio

Chapter Nine

"Can We Come Too?"—Around Town or Around the World — Traveling with Multiples

Whether you are traveling across town or across continents, traveling with your babies can be fun or it can be a disaster. Your method of travel, your destination, and your personal expectations of the trip all will influence the final outcome. We have heard from parents who rarely leave their neighborhoods and parents who have crossed the globe, and they all say the same thing:

TIP!

Go into the experience with an open mind. You will get there eventually.

Bill says, "Load 'em up and go! Take the dog too!" I prefer to leave the dog behind, but even my threshold levels are slowly adapting. Find the threshold that works for you. Don't overdo it, otherwise everyone suffers.

Be flexible, and you will set a lifetime example for the children to be flexible too.

"It's a Beautiful Day in the Neighborhood"—Traveling by Foot

If you are just out in the neighborhood or at a local park, strollers and wagons work pretty well:

- ❋ If your children are old enough, try a large Little Tikes wagon; people might think you're sitting for a several families' kids.

- ❋ Step 2 makes a four-by-two-foot wagon that has a "tag-along" attaching wagon, perfect for two or three and all their stuff.

- ❋ If you are out shopping in a mall, a whole different set of dynamics come into play. First of all, there is no question that a twin or triplet stroller draws attention.

If you ever have a bad day and need some adult contact, load the babies into the stretch-limo stroller, meander leisurely through the mall, and watch what happens. But if you're not up for being bombarded with attention, your outing can eat up your precious time. An errand which might otherwise take forty-five minutes turns into ninety minutes as you deal with the rush of questions from fascinated strangers and well-meaning neighbors. This phenomenon is more intense when they are infants.

> *"The worst thing for me was being constantly stopped in the stores and even having people ask me to 'wait here while I get my husband'.... I was easily stopped by thirty people or more on every trip, and that adds an hour to the shopping—not a pleasant prospect when you have three babies getting tired and hungry. What I wanted to do was to type up a paper stating basically, 'Yes, they are triplets. Yes, I am proud of my children and would love to show them to everybody, but time does not allow me this'; and then answer all the typical questions (names, ages, birth weights, etc.)."*
>
> **—DB, Puxico, Mo.**

Still, a trip to the local shopping mall is great exercise and diversion, especially in poor weather, so don't let all the attention stop you. And remember, generally speaking, people's intentions are good. Here are some tips to help you and your babies enjoy your outing:

- Pick a time when you're up for it, otherwise don't go. If you're frustrated or angry, this will intensify the negative experience.

- Accept the fact that you will draw attention and will be delayed. Enjoy it, and be proud of your magnificent children.

- Target your shopping sprees around the least busy times. Early Sunday mornings are a breeze in the grocery stores.

- Triplet strollers are dead giveaways. Take someone with you and use two strollers, one single and one double. Fewer eyes will notice your children and you can get your business done with little distraction.

- Take your sitter along with the triplet stroller, and let your sitter stroll the store while you price diapers and supplies. The sitter usually enjoys the attention it draws, and you can get your shopping done without the interruptions.

- Don't dress them alike. This will only attract more attention and intensify curiosity.

- Carry your keys and essentials in a fannypack strapped around your waist to keep your hands free.

- When the children get a bit older, give them their own backpacks to carry their own stuff in. Generally, this really appeals to them and they love all the zippers and compartments.

> "There are wonderful grocery carts that are made for three children. They must be able to sit up before you can use them, but these carts have made my life so much easier! I don't have to deal with the triplet stroller at the grocery store anymore!"
>
> —TG, Mentor, Ohio

SHARE THE JOY AND BRAGGING RIGHTS

Another interesting phenomenon that occurs is the attachment of semi-strangers—such as the grocery store clerk, the pharmacist, or the mailman—to your babies. These well-meaning people may not know your name, but they will take on harmless bragging rights to your children. Often we would walk in the store and the store manager would say, "Oh, here come our Toys R Us triplets!" Another lesson our babies have taught us is to share the joy they have brought into our lives.

"Buckle Up!"—Traveling by Car

Planning ahead and having realistic expectations are keys to successful road trips. Remember, getting there should be half the fun. It won't be long before every two seconds they ask, "Are we there yet?"

❖ For short trips to the store or while running errands, be prepared to bail out at any time. Babies have a way of hitting the wall before you're ready to go home.

> "Be prepared for the mutiny—it can strike at any time!"
> —**Bill, Behind the Wheel**

❖ For long trips, don't expect to reach your destination at a particular time. If you leave at noon and estimate a five-hour drive, you will not arrive at 5:00 P.M. You will get there when you get there.

> "Our first car trip was fifteen hours long. We stopped at every McDonald's and got french fries."
> —**JB, University Heights, Ohio**

❖ Try timing your adventures around their sleep schedules, and don't forget the snacks!

❖ Make the van an extension of your home, and keep it stocked with supplies.

"Start off close to their naptime so they will sleep. We stopped at least every four hours to stretch. Fortunately, our experience was great. They did well. Lots of toys, singing, and snacks."

—KD, N. Olmstead, Ohio

"When our three were infants we drove from Cincinnati to Wisconsin to Massachusetts and back home to Ohio. We survived this trip in part because we traveled at night. For feedings we carried a cooler with cans of formula concentrate and a thermos of hot water. Diluting the formula concentrate half and half with the hot water resulted in the perfect temperature for a Happy Meal on the road."

—LL, Morrow, Ohio

"Keep a fully-stocked diaper bag with you at all times. Being away from home without diapers is like being in the desert without water."

—Dr. RP, Shaker Heights, Ohio

"Keep a stash of diapers, wipes, supplies, snacks, and toys in the van. You never know when you might want to accomplish an extra errand or when you might find yourself sitting in traffic."

—Bill the Diaper Master

❖ Eliminate, or at least reduce, the car seat wrestling matches by permanently assigning each child to a seat early on, and stick with it.

"Assign your children a seat forever!"

—BT, N. Olmstead, Ohio

❖ A luggage carrier for the top of the van is great for hauling all your baby paraphernalia. It stores things out of sight and gives you the extra room you need to move around inside the van until you reach your destination.

✖ Bring along your portable six-panel play-yards to corral all the children in one baby-safe place. They're flexible and can be rendered into different shapes and sizes, creating blockades or pens, indoors and out.

> *"We kept a playpen in the garage and used it as a staging area for loading and unloading the van. Throw in a few toys to keep the babies occupied while you load and unload the groceries."*
> —**Sheila in Process**

✖ Rent a small trailer and pack it full of your stuff—toys, coolers, portable cribs, and supplies—and pull it behind your van. The extra room inside the van is great, and you will be able to move around inside the van more easily. On long hauls, stop every couple of hours and break out some food and toys from the trailer.

> *"In our minivan, the three-seater seat can slide up behind the front seat. It is great for vacations, because all kids are an arm's length away and there is more room in the rear."*
> —**KD, N. Olmstead, Ohio**

✖ Rent an RV. Recreational vehicles provide all the conveniences of home, including running water, and give a sense of camping in the outdoors.

✖ Bring along sidewalk chalk for any stops in between.

✖ Purchase a TV/VCR for the van. Also purchase videos (new or used) that the children have not seen. You'll literally get a lot of miles out of them.

✖ Keep a special stash of toys for long drives. Fresh new toys or books will keep them entertained and occupied for longer stretches of time.

✖ Remember, whether it's a trip across town or across the country, the vehicle doesn't move unless everyone is buckled safely in their car seat. It is far better to stop frequently and arrive late than to make an exception to the car seat rule that could put your precious babies at risk.

"Planning Is Everything!"—Traveling by Air

Airports are like busy ant colonies. They are filled with hurried people on cell phones with places to go and people to meet. Airline personnel are focused on processing people in an effort to meet their "on time" schedules. Whatever assistance you do get from the airlines, consider it a bonus.

Most people will be oblivious to you and your children. Those who do take note tend to watch you struggle as you negotiate tight turns with all your babies and their paraphernalia. Then the *"Are they natural?"* questions begin.

First Things First—Reserve Your Seats Well In Advance

Advise the airline that you are traveling with multiple babies or small children. The number of tickets you will need to purchase depends on the age of your children, how comfortable you want to be, and seating configurations on the aircraft. If your children are under the age of two they are considered "lap babies" and can fly for free. Each child must sit on the lap of one adult for the entire flight.

This means that if you have three lap babies you need three adults. If you are lucky and the flight is not sold out, you can use the empty seat next to you to spread out. But don't count on this! Most flights in the major markets are full and often over-sold; chances are you will not have an empty seat next to you.

If you are traveling with a lap baby, the number of oxygen masks available per row will dictate where you and your children can sit. On domestic flights, federal aviation law allows only two lap babies per entire row. A row is defined as all the seats across which are divided by the aisle! This is because the aircraft has only one extra oxygen mask above each seating group, and in the case of an emergency, everyone, including baby, must have an oxygen mask available to them. This means only two lap babies per entire row. In the case of triplets or more, you will have to sit in separate rows.

Reserve your seats around this FAA law. It's best to select seats that are in front of or behind each other. This way you can pass stuff back and forth easily, and you get to hold the babies up over the tops of the seats and play peek-a-boo. This seating arrangement works great for twins, too. If you don't take this measure, you will find yourself in a last minute, on-board seating shuffle.

Domestic flights usually have two seating groups per row divided by an aisle.

Three and Three	Two and Three
XXX Aisle XXX	XX Aisle XXX

International flights generally have three seating clusters per row with two aisles dividing the seating groups. The best advice is to reserve well in advance and notify the ticket agent of your situation.

XX Aisle XXXXX Aisle XX
XXX Aisle XXX Aisle XXX

Remember! There is only one extra oxygen mask per seating group.

"Should I Buy Extra Seats?"

A good rule of thumb is, if the flight is two hours or more, bite the bullet and buy the extra seat for each child even if they qualify as a lap baby. Airlines will usually sell the seat for half the price of an adult fare. In this case, you don't have to be concerned about the location of oxygen masks, the aircraft's seating configurations, and any other surprises such as a last minute change in aircraft, which happens frequently. Your flight will be more expensive, but it is well worth it. Now you can lift up the armrest between the seats and lay the babies down for a nap. You and your children will be more comfortable and less stressed.

If you intend to keep the babies in their car seats during flight, you will have to buy a seat for each one of them.

Coach Seats Are Better Than First Class

You're probably thinking, "huh?" Even if you can afford first class tickets for your instantly expanded family, consider coach for one reason. The armrest. The armrest in first class doesn't lift up between the seats and in coach it does! If you have purchased the seat next to you, or you lucked out and it's empty, you can lift up the armrest between the two seats and one of babies can sleep lying down, and you can sit back and enjoy your peanuts!

The armrest in first class does not lift up.

"How Many Adults Should Assist When Flying with Multiples?"

One adult per child is the recommended ratio. This means two laps for two babies, three laps for three babies, four laps for four.

If you have one extra adult, all the better; taking turns makes the trip so much easier.

If you have one fewer adult, you can bring a car seat to strap into a seat for the extra child, but of course you will have to buy that seat.

> *"At least one adult per child is a must! It is too risky to travel with any fewer adults. Just the security issues alone are huge! In a busy airport, your attention will be repeatedly diverted from the children during check-in, boarding, baggage claim, car rental procedures, map-reading, and more. It is too easy for a child to toddle away."*
>
> **—KR, Wadsworth, Ohio**

IN-FLIGHT NEEDS—"IT'S ALWAYS SOMETHING"

When traveling with several babies, something always comes up. Remember, when traveling with multiples, go into the experience with an open mind and prepare to be flexible. They will either sleep most of the flight or not.

FIRST ON—LAST OFF

The airline will allow you to board the aircraft before the other passengers, so you can get settled without having to rush or hold up others. This takes a large amount of stress right out of the picture. You can wheel your strollers right down the jet way and the gate agent will check your strollers as luggage as you board the aircraft.

Wait until everyone else de-planes before you and your family do. You will have to wait for your strollers that were gate-checked anyway, so you might as well sit back and wait until you have the elbow-room to assemble everyone and everything.

TAKE-OFF AND LANDING

It's a great idea for the babies to suck bottles or pacifiers upon take-off and landing to equalize the pressure in their ears due to the change in the cabin's air pressure.

HEATING UP MILK

If you run short of milk, relax; there is plenty of fresh milk on board. If you want to heat up the milk in flight, try using the plastic-coated airsickness bag. The fight attendant can fill them with hot water and place the bottles inside for a quick warm-up.

MEALS

When making your reservation you can order special children's meals. They usually offer old-time favorites such as peanut butter and jelly sandwiches, hot dogs, hamburgers, chicken nuggets, cereal, and fruit.

CHANGING DIAPERS MID-FLIGHT

Not a problem. You are diaper changing artists by now, and you can change a diaper just about anywhere, and that includes right there in the seat. If it is a messy one or you want a little more privacy, some of the larger aircrafts have changing tables in the lavatories. If not, you can put the toilet seat down and use it as a changing surface. In either case, airline lavatories are not clean places, so cover the changing surface with a blanket.

> *"If you want to create a big mess and attract a lot of attention, pour the milk on their cereal. If not, let them eat the cereal dry with their hands, and pour the milk in their sippy cups. Hide the fruit and give it to them as a snack later."*
>
> —**Bill and the Bunch at 30,000 Feet**

KEEPING THEM OCCUPIED

As they get older, it takes more to keep them entertained and occupied. Don't expect your little ones to sit back and enjoy the scenery.

TIP!

New scenery to them means countless trips to the bathroom!

Bring along their favorite toys, blankets, and books, or consider buying something shiny and new that will capture their attention for longer stretches of time. It's also a good idea to hold back a small stash of some particularly tempting trinkets or treats in case of those "hairy moments" or an unexpected delay.

"Bring a bag of snacks and toys they haven't seen. Hand them out as necessary."
—JB, University Heights, Ohio

And a few more tips:

❈ In-flight Kiddie Kits are usually available from the airline in the summer, when the vacation travel season is at its peak. They are filled with little flight wings, games, small globes, and other things that will help keep your toddlers occupied.

❈ Many airports have play areas on the concourses. If you have a layover, check with a ground agent to find out where on the concourse they are located.

❈ The pilot will let children have a courtesy visit in the cockpit before or after the flight, not during. This may not appeal to your young toddlers, but it sure is fun for us grown-ups!

TIP!

If you can afford it, arrange to bring one of your sitters. Free travel and lodging as well as a financial bonus will usually be an ample incentive for the sitter to help care for and entertain the children. This helps make the trip more enjoyable for everyone.

- Sitting still is difficult for children. If at all possible, make time for active play before, during, and after the trip to help use up some of that pent-up energy.

A Screaming Child in Flight

When walking down the aisle to your seats, the looks on the other passengers' faces are really funny.

> *"The theme song from 'Jaws' is pounding through their heads, getting louder and louder as you approach them. As you pass on by, you hear the sighs of relief."*
>
> **—Kyle and Crew, Gilbert, Ariz.**

We interviewed several flight attendants on the subject of a screaming baby in flight, and they shared their insights with us. Their observations indicate that the parent or caregiver traveling with the screaming baby is more stressed about it than anyone else on the plane (other than the baby). It's important to know that most other passengers are sympathetic and understanding of the situation. So don't worry yourself with what others are thinking, because most are in your court. It is the very few who will be demonstratively annoyed by your baby's cry.

> *"It was a full flight... we were the last to board, and the flight attendant was trying to rush us to take our seats. While we were trying to get three children fastened into their seats, suddenly my son began to SCREAM!!! 'I want to sit next to Mommy'; the usual screaming fit. Yes, we created quite a scene. People were staring at us and loudly sighing as this three-year-old got louder and louder. My husband all of a sudden held our son high enough for everyone to see and said, 'Everyone, I would like you to meet my son Christopher, he is the one making all of the noise and creating a scene on this airplane. I am not a bad parent!' When our son realized people were staring at him he was a bit embarrassed and quickly stopped screaming. Everyone found this quite humorous and began laughing. Rather than everyone disliking us and commenting on how misbehaved our son was, they all left the airplane laughing and politely saying good-bye to Christopher. I have no idea what possessed my husband to do this, but it worked. I would recommend this for anyone traveling with a screaming child."*
>
> **—CS, Algonquin, Ill.**
> **The Triplet Connection**

Take this advice to heart, because you should be commended for taking on the challenge of traveling with multiples. And remember, like everything else, the crying will eventually stop. Bon voyage and enjoy your flight!

VAN OR CAR RENTAL

When you reserve your vehicle, also reserve car seats. They all have car seats available to rent. Some agencies will provide one or all free of charge. It doesn't hurt to ask if they will "throw in" the car seats. They usually do.

The larger sedans like the Taurus and the luxury vehicles are big enough to accommodate three car seats in the back seat. They are cheaper to rent than a van but you don't get the extra room you probably will need for all of your baby stuff, including that stroller.

CREATING A HOME AWAY FROM HOME

Staying away from home can seem a little daunting, especially when you think of all the stuff it takes feed, clothe, and entertain your little ones. With a little preparation and creativity, however, you can create an environment that will provide just the right combination of diversion and security for you and the babies.

✦ Look for a "Baby's Away" rental. This great service is offered in over thirty locations across the United States. They rent and deliver almost any baby equipment imaginable to your hotel, condo, or cabin—you name it. Located mostly in vacation and resort destinations, they eliminate the hassle of hauling along all the awkward and cumbersome, but necessary, baby paraphernalia that you need when you are away from home. They offer service twenty-four hours a day, seven days a week. (See Chapter 14.)

✦ Portable cribs and playpens are all terrific products that the children can sleep in when away from home. They are compact and portable.

"A Trunk Full of Tips"—Other Travel Tips

VISITING RELATIVES

❋ If you are visiting relatives, call ahead and give them a basic shopping list of essential groceries you will need upon arrival. Then you don't have to pack them or go through the shopping drill once you arrive after a long, exhausting trip.

❋ Ask your relatives to borrow or rent any large equipment for you to use during your stay: high chairs, playpens, booster seats.

❋ Relatives don't always remember how to baby-proof the house. Avoid stress and potential discord, not to mention potential hazards to the children, by bringing in the portable play-yard to create a "baby safe" zone.

HOTELS

❋ If staying at a hotel, call ahead early and reserve cribs. They may not always have them but booking early can help. Call the hotel itself (not the 1-800 reservation number) two hours before you arrive to request that they be set up and ready to go when you arrive. Otherwise, you can find yourself waiting in the minivan with a bunch of exhausted kids for two hours while the hotel housekeeping staff gets around to cleaning and setting up your room.

❋ Hotels have to conform to fire code laws which do not allow more than five people in a regular room. With twins, triplets, or other siblings, plus Mom and Dad, you can be in violation, and will require two rooms. If so, get a double occupancy rate and connecting rooms if possible.

❋ Get adjoining rooms and set up all the cribs and baby stuff in one room and designate the other as the adult room. CAUTION: Be sure to have the keys to access both rooms in your pocket *at all times.*

IT HAPPENED TO US!

Baby Austin slammed the interior connecting door shut behind him. We were horrified to discover that he and all the keys were locked inside the room. While Austin ran wild and unattended inside with the TV blaring, Bill scaled the balcony trying to gain access through the exterior patio door. I called security. Finally, the cavalry arrived and hotel security unlocked the door.

❧ Childproof your hotel rooms by placing coffee tables, plants, and other hazards in the closets. Drape towels over the tops of closet and bathroom doors to prevent their fingers from becoming caught.

❧ Place one of the mattresses on the floor in the corner and pack extra pillows around it for the babies to sleep on. If there isn't an extra mattress in the room, lay several large blankets on the floor and have a slumber party.

> *"Remake one double bed so all three triplets can sleep across it together."*
>
> **—BL, Chagrin Falls, Ohio**

❧ Bring along a night-light so if one awakes in the middle of the night you won't stumble into everything in the dark and wake everyone else up.

❧ Bring one car seat, walker, or exersaucer into the room and feed one child at a time. This minimizes the hassle of hauling equipment in and out of the vehicle and takes up less space inside the room.

❧ If you have access to the concierge or upgrade lounges, use them!

❧ Many full-service Holiday Inn Hotels have "Holidomes." Holidomes offer indoor playgrounds, mini-put-put, baby pools, and game rooms surrounded by places for adults to sit and relax while watching the children. These are great local and inexpensive getaways, especially in the winter, if you live in a cold climate.

Chapter Eleven

"Quick, Give Me an Idea, FAST!"

Parents of multiples, by necessity, learn to parent smarter. Ingenuity, inventiveness, creativity, and humor are just some of the skills they use to get through the day. Read on!

Time Savers!

- When possible, stay one step ahead by setting up in advance.
- Prepare the day's meals early in the morning or the night before.
- If it saves on trips up and down the stairs, bathe the babies in the kitchen sink until they no longer fit. Chances are, you'll take some great photos of them in the sink!
- Grocery shopping services can be a lifesaver, especially if you are alone. They will buy what's on your list and deliver right to your door.
- Keep a continuous grocery list, so when someone offers to pick something up for you, you'll know quickly what you need.

"Set the next meal up right after you finish cleaning up the last one. When they're all screaming at once, ready for their next meal of mashed bananas and Cheerios, you'll be ready to go."

—Ready-Set-Go Sheila

"Set up whatever you can in advance, i.e., set out clothes, set the table, and set up for meals in advance. Make oatmeal the night before, keep it in the fridge for a quick warm-up in the morning."

—BT, N. Olmstead, Ohio

"Set up stations around your house where you spend most of your time with diapers, wipes, ointments, clippers, and so forth all within hands reach."

—TG, Mentor, Ohio

"Keep a diaper bag packed with essentials in your car and you're ready to go."

—TG, Mentor, Ohio

"For baths, get everything you need set up before starting."

—KD, N. Olmstead, Ohio

"We use pool slippers or 'water-socks' around the house as shoes to cover their feet. They slip on and off quickly. When we go outside we put on the real shoes."

—Bill

"Keep a running grocery list on your fridge, and use your crock pot—just throw your dinner in and let your crock pot do the work."

—TG, Mentor, Ohio

CRIB SHEETS

This is a great way to save time and energy and add some pizzazz to the nursery!

- ❇ Pull the entire mattress out of the crib when changing the babies' crib sheets. It's so much easier and faster than wrestling with the sheets and the corners of the mattress while hunched over the crib rails.

- ❇ Waterproof pads in the cribs save tremendously on the number of trips to the laundry room.

> *"Crib sheets… my guys have figured how to pull them off the mattresses! I bought a bunch of knit T- shirt material on sale (cheap, colorful, washes great, feels good too!). It comes in a tube form. I just cut it into lengths (about five feet per bed) stitched one end closed and hemmed the other and now 'slipcover' the mattress. They are easy to get on and off. When I am desperate, I flip the mattress over. All for about three dollars apiece."*
>
> **—NS, Baton Rouge, La.**
> **The Triplet Connection**

VELCRO IS KING!

For parents of multiples, Velcro deserves it's own place in the Smithsonian. For everyday dressing and feeding:

- ❇ Velcro bibs are fast and easy. Snaps are OK, but ties are out of the question!!

- ❇ Velcro straps on shoes—no laces. Chances are you'll be putting on the same shoes over and over, all day long.

- ❇ Velcro on their jackets—zippers take forever.

HASSLE-FREE DRIVE-UPS

They may not have the soup du jour, but drive-up windows at convenience stores are great for picking up the essentials, such as milk and bread. Drive-up pharmacies are fantastic. No need to get out of the minivan and deal with that stroller.

> **TIP!**
>
> **The less you have to unbuckle…, lift…, situate…, buckle…, stroll…, unbuckle…, lift again…, and rebuckle times XXX, the better!**

COLORED ICE CREAM CONES

- They may all get the same flavor ice cream, but let them pick out their favorite color cone.

- Use colored cones as edible cups to hold snacks—this means less clean-up!

One-Stop Shopping

CATALOGS AND INTERNET

Catalogs remain the most popular way to shop from home, but as people become increasingly Internet-savvy, online shopping is right on their heels.

The most popular catalogs today are:

JC Penney Catalog

Spiegel Catalog

Fingerhut Catalog

Baby Catalog of America

If you shop online, check to see if you're getting a competitive price by visiting www.bargains.org. This is a nonprofit Web site that examines what target prices should be and will allow you to compare prices and determine if you're overpaying or if you're getting a good deal.

Whether you prefer catalogs or online shopping, make sure you understand the company's return policy before you place your order.

"If It Glows In the Dark, Buy It"

- Bright florescent colors for sippy cups will help you find them later, when the babies drop or stash them in obscure places.

- Bright-colored clothing helps your eyes spot your children during large family gatherings or multiples' playgroups, as the children bounce off each other like little molecules.

For Toddlers Who Are Picky Eaters

- If they don't like the sound of it, change the name! Make up fun names like "Lion Food" or "Monster Meat."

- Let them participate in meal selection. If you're brave enough, let them help in meal preparation!

- Whoever gets to cut the pie gets served last. This guarantees that the pieces will be sliced with the precision of a surgeon and reduces fighting over who got the bigger piece.

- Use cookie cutters to create fun shapes for cheese, lunch meats, or Jell-O. Get creative and make faces on sandwiches using carrot circles or hard boiled egg circles for eyes and noses.

- A few drops of food coloring literally changes the picture. Kids like gross things such as red pancakes and blue mashed potatoes.

- Hide the vegetables inside other foods or in fruit yogurt.

- Create healthy shakes in the blender with any combination of fruit, yogurt, tofu, ice, milk, or ice cream. What doesn't get finished can go in the freezer for tomorrow.

- Discover dips! Kids love dips, and they will make their own concoctions. Use empty egg carton trays as dipping stations and fill them with ketchup, cheese sauce, sweet and sour, yogurt, spaghetti sauce, you name it.

- Turn off the TV during meals.

Space Savers

We don't have very much to say about saving space. Multiples have a way of taking over.

- Put up shelves in the nursery, the nursery closet, and the laundry room.

- Bunk cribs—if you can find them.

- Bunk beds—when ready.

"The action is non-stop— eat, play, fuss, diaper change, play, fuss, snacks, naps, eat, play. Our entire house is triplet territory. Thoroughly baby-proofed, it looks like a day care center laden with baby equipment and toys."

—Non-Stop Sheila

- Loft beds—create a new play zone in addition to sleeping areas.

- Trundle beds—for after they transition from cribs.

- Stash infant carriers under cribs.

- Convert the top of a large dresser into a changing table. All you need is a pad and a handy supply of diapers and wipes.

- Keep only the clothes that fit today in their room. Keep clothes that you bought or received that don't fit today in a storage area. Periodically rotate.

"If you don't use it— don't keep it! Don't be a storage warehouse manager in addition to being a parent of supertwins."

—Bill

- ✖ Purge your house of things you don't use and don't need and have a big garage sale.

- ✖ Use clear plastic bins, laundry baskets, or plastic milk crates to stash related items.

- ✖ If necessary, forget about parking your car in the garage. Convert your garage into a living or storage space.

- ✖ Utilize your closets to their fullest. Create shelving systems, and keep all of the children's toys in large plastic containers or boxes and store by category: cars in one box, stuffed animals in another, etc. Teach the children that they must put away the toys from one box before they are allowed to take out toys from another box.

- ✖ Use cabana-style curtains to cover open shelving. They can be tied back when shelving is in use.

"To keep track of shoes we hung a three-tier wire basket (the type used in the kitchen) in the girls' room. They can't reach it and the shoes don't get lost. The wire basket is also good for baby lotion, powder, wipes, etc. when the kids are younger."

—KP, Bay Shore, N.Y.
The Triplet Connection

"Put the dresser in the closet."

— NJ, Macedonia, Ohio

"Often, because of the slope of the stairs, the ceiling height of a closet is too low for normal adult use. But it's a perfect height if you happen to be less than three feet tall. It makes a perfect playhouse for the children and stores their many toys."

—Bill, The Cave Dweller

Clean-Up Tips

"Get a dog
named Hoover!"

—LS, Columbus, Ohio

"You can't match the
gratifying feeling when
you see your German
short-hair pointer clean
up the latest cracker
feeding better than the
best wet-dry vac."

—KT, Gilbert, Ariz.
The Triplet Connection

"Now all we have to find
is a good carpet cleaner."

—Kyle and Crew, Gilbert, Ariz.

"Clean-up? What's that?
Coming from a former
neat-freak."

—BT, N. Olmstead, Ohio

"Wash down the high chairs
with the hose outside!"

—JB, Birmingham, Ala.

"Place a twin sheet on the
floor under the high chairs.
After eating I shake it off
outside and then throw it
in the washer."

—ET, Belleville, Ill.
The Triplet Connection

"I kept a plastic bowl by
the kitchen sink to put
dirty bottle nipples and
rings in. I rinsed them off
before dropping them in,
making it easy and effi-
cient for clean-up."

—LL, Beeville, Tex.
The Triplet Connection

"An oblong, flannel-
backed vinyl tablecloth
has many uses. Vinyl side
up it's a changing pad to
hold all three or a carpet
cover under the high
chairs. Flannel side up,
it's a waterproof pad
during potty training at
night or for naps on
grandma's bed."

—SE, Roseburg, Ore.
The Triplet Connectiom

Odors

You probably don't want to know what that odor is. Elmo tends to have a distinct smell after being in the oven at 350 degrees. Here are some ways keep the odors under control.

- Try fabric softener sheets in the diaper pail, they keep the odors down.
- Don't forget to wash the peanut butter from behind their ears!
- Make sure they wear socks with their shoes. They don't make "odor-eaters" that small.

Photo Tips

"I always tried to have the babies lined up according to birth order—oldest on the left, etc. That way I could distinguish each of them at a glance."

—RW, Aurora, Col.
The Triplet Connection

"When we receive clothing gifts, we try to take a picture of the babies in their new outfit and send the photo to the person who gave us the gift."

—Sheila

"When the babies were first born, I had so many requests for pictures that I gave away some of my best originals and did not have a chance to make reprints. Now when I take my film in to be developed, I ask for two copies. Once I receive the pictures, I quickly date the backs. When I have time, I can add more details and can put them in chronological order."

—RW, Aurora, Col.
The Triplet Connection

> "I've taken pictures on their birthday each month during the first year. In the picture, I have a sign listing name, age, month, and any other milestones met that month. The signs are made of construction paper and are sometimes held by big brother, taped to high chairs or walkers, or propped against furniture."
>
> —JC, Arnold, Mo.
> **The Triplet Connection**

Quick Tips!

⚡ Kitchen garbage bags are too big for diaper pails. To make it fit securely, pinch two inches along the top edge of the bag and tie a knot, reducing the diameter at the top of the bag. Drop the bag into the pail and gently stretch the top of the bag around the rim of the pail.

⚡ Keep your house and car keys in a designated place at all times.

⚡ Steam a one-pound bag of raw baby carrots. They keep well and are a nutritious food for the babies and a great snack food for you to eat on-the-go!

⚡ When cooking for you and your partner, prepare two meals at one time, freezing one.

⚡ Play-yards—encircle the living room, encircle the entire downstairs, encircle the whole house!

⚡ Take one baby with you when running errands and leave the other two at home with a sitter. It's easier for everyone to manage.

⚡ If you're getting ready for an outing, put their shoes on while they're still sitting in their high chairs—fast and easy!

⚡ In cool weather, a shortcut to getting to the store is to leave the babies in their sleepers and put a pair of sweat pants and a coat over them. This works best in the first year before the babies walk and need shoes. One more thing, be sure the sleepers are the type with feet so your little darlings don't get cold feet.

✖ Hook retractable dog leashes to their belt loops to keep your racing toddlers out of trouble when you are out.

"Grandma and Grandpa Are Going to Just Love It!"

For grandparents and other relatives who live out of town, there are many innovative ways to share your babies' development and joy.

"Stencil a cookie jar cover with a set of the babies' handprints. Make a batch of cookies using a cookie cutter in the shape of small hands and fill the jar!"

—KR, Wadsworth, Ohio

"I use three colored crayons so we know who 'signed' cards for grandparents."

—PA, The Triplet Connection

WEAR THEM!

"A great present for grandma is to purchase a white sweatshirt and some pink or blue stenciling paint. I painted my girls' hands, sparingly, and pressed them onto the shirt. I also included my oldest child, who loved to be involved in the project. After the shirt had dried, I cross-stitched the girls' names and ages under their hands and presented it to my mother-in-law. She is so proud to 'wear' her girls. If you are very adventurous, why not put their feet on the back! Remember, the trick is not to put too much paint on—go easy!"

—MR, Ferndale, Mich.
The Triplet Connection

Brag Bag!

Extend this stencil idea to a plain cotton tote bag found at most arts and crafts stores. Using fabric paint, make handprints on one side and footprints on the other.

Tape Them!

- Make videotapes of a typical day in the life of your babies. Record waking up, mealtime, naptime, playtime, bath time, getting ready for bed, and the giggles and fusses in between.
- If you don't own a video camera, rent or borrow one. This is a great gift that will be remembered for a long time.
- Include an individual-size package of microwave popcorn to add to the fun!
- Ask grandma and grandpa to send a tape of themselves in return. The kids will love it!

Bookmarks

How about taking those extra photos, cutting out the babies' faces, and taping them on strips of colorful posterboard? Then take them to your local copy store and have them laminated into personalized bookmarks.

"When they're young, keep a hand-held tape recorder nearby so you can record the babies' coos, gurgles, screeches, and all the noises they make. Capture them vocalizing individually or when they're all chiming in like a choir. Make a copy and give it to grandma and grandpa, but don't tell them what it is. Enclose a note to listen to this while driving in their car."

—Bill and the Babies

"We wrote baby update letters to family and friends. Whoever came and stayed with us—grandparents, aunts, etc., we encouraged to write a paragraph about their experiences with each baby. My sisters sent the letters out for me. This helped keep the phone calls to a minimum at a busy time, and everyone loved being able to share our experiences. The letters are a wonderful account of what life was like that first year, and our triplets will love reading them when they are older."

—CB, Linden, Calif.
The Triplet Connection

Chapter Twelve

"It's Gonna Take More Than Sit-Ups"— Tummy Tucks

The Costs and the Benefits

Eight months after my delivery, despite all the sit-ups I could manage and a good diet, my abdomen was still a disaster area. The muscular separation of my abdominal wall looked like the *Grand Canyon!!* My abdominal skin looked like the knee of an elephant! To make things worse, when I sat up my guts would pop through the deep herniated crevasse. I was doomed.

> **TIP!**
>
> **I guess this was my badge of honor for carrying all of my babies at once. But I had been stretched beyond the point of no return.**

Even though I was back to my pre-pregnancy weight, I knew my belly would never be the same. In fact, I was stronger and in better physical shape than ever, thanks to constantly lifting my little ones and climbing the "stairmaster to babyland," up and down the stairs to the nursery twenty-four hours a day. It was true. I had a ventral hernia and my hanging blob of jelly was here to stay.

With the assault on your abdomen you may want to consider an abdominoplasty, most commonly known as a "tummy tuck."

> **TIP!**
>
> **But wait! Whoever named it a "tummy tuck" obviously has not had one.**

This is a *major* surgical procedure that removes excess skin and fat from the middle and lower abdomen and surgically tightens the muscles of the separated abdominal wall. You will come home dangling drainage tubes from your belly, swollen like a watermelon, bound with a very tight corset, and hunched over for four to six weeks. Your abdominal skin will be stretched tight as a drum, and you won't be able to stand up straight.

> **TIP!**
>
> **You'll feel like you have a giant rubber band over your neck and down to your toes as your stitched muscles and taut skin slowly start to stretch back.**

But the results are fantastic and you also get a new belly button!

A tuck involves a long recovery period, and you will not be able lift anything, including the little basketball team that got you into this shape to begin with! Don't underestimate the recuperation period! Plan for help during this time.

One thing is for sure: a tuck will dramatically reduce the appearance of a protruding abdomen. It will also leave a permanent "smiley scar" extending from hip to hip. For some women, a partial abdominoplasty may be in order; others may require a full abdominoplasty in conjunction with liposuction. Of course, consult with a qualified plastic surgeon who can inform you of the risks, alternatives, and recovery time, and help set realistic expectations of the end results.

TIP!   **The national average cost for an abdominoplasty is $3,000 to $5,000.**

Health insurance policies typically do not cover abdomino-plasty costs; however, in the case of a multiple birth pregnancy, everything is exaggerated, including the severe muscular damage to your abdominal wall. Some women have been successful getting their insurance companies to cover the costs. Some insurance companies will cover the reconstruction of the abdominal wall but classify the removal of the excess skin as cosmetic. The choice is yours!

"I felt like I had a new wardrobe! I can say it has been worth it! I can wear clothes that I haven't been able to wear in the past four years (since the birth of my singleton four years ago and triplets two years ago.) I feel good in a bathing suit, although I had to be careful picking out a few suits because of the hip to hip scar. Overall, I would definitely recommend this surgery. The results are fantastic and the short-lived pain is worth it."

—JB, Birmingham, Ala.

"The money I spent on my tummy tuck would have sooner or later been spent on a new wardrobe. Now my abdomen is flat as a board, and I can wear all my clothes again! The only problem is that now hemlines are changing again, oh well!"

—Sheila Goes Shopping

Chapter Thirteen

"I Miss the Kids Already and They're Only Sleeping"

Reflections

Watching them grow up together is awesome. We ponder with wonderment that they have been together from the first spark of life. We know that they will always be together somehow, regardless of any physical distance between them and even in death. To be a multiple is so special.

At night when they're all in bed, all we talk about is what they did that day, how they interacted with each other, and what they learned. We talk about how lucky we are and what they taught us, too! Your children will teach you valuable lessons about life over and over.

TIP! Some of the lessons they will teach you will not be so obvious and others will stop you in your tracks.

But in the end, like it was in the beginning, there is just a feeling of awe. It's because of them you can now do anything. Everything else is easy.

It's all how you look at it. These first few years are hard, hard work, but take it in stride. Eventually you'll get some, but not all, of your life back. Just look at what you get in return!

Our children have broadened our perspective and helped us understand some of our true potential. We have been able to go beyond our perceived limitations and we often say to ourselves, "If I can do this, everything else is easy."

> *"If you watch them sleep at night you realize how incredibly lucky you are to be a parent. I love watching them go through new experiences. It is like reliving your own childhood."*
>
> —JB, University Heights, Ohio

> *"Sometimes when I'm in an airport, putting out several brush fires through a daisy chain of voice mails during the final boarding call, I giggle and say to myself, 'No sweat, this is nothing. You're looking at a woman who is raising triplets! This is a walk in the park.'"*
>
> —Sheila

> *"They bring neighborhoods and communities together, build new friendships, and even help heal the bumpy ones that needed a little TLC."*
>
> —Angelene Laut, Grandmother to Our Children

> *"We love watching them all fall down in a heap before the cue when singing 'Ring Around The Rosie.'"*
>
> —Sheila and Bill

> *"Stop and smell the roses—life is too short to put anything but your children first."*
>
> —BT, N. Olmstead, Ohio

> "All we have to do is look
> into the rear-view mirror
> of the minivan and see
> three shining faces
> looking back."
>
> —**Sheila and Bill**

> "Spoil them with
> your time, not with
> material things."
>
> —**BT, N. Olmstead, Ohio**

> "They have taught me to be
> patient, creative, loving,
> and compassionate, and I
> am a better person because
> of them— a little frazzled
> at times— but a much
> better person!"
>
> —**TG, Mentor, Ohio**

> "Happiness is a journey,
> not a destination.
>
> Work like you don't need
> the money,
>
> Love like you've never
> been hurt,
>
> And dance like no one's
> watching."
>
> —**Note from the Marshall Islands by
> way of a Triplet Father in Arizona**

> "The best part of having
> multiples is all the love
> that comes at once."
>
> —**BT, N. Olmstead, Ohio**

Hope Chests

An extra-special gift for your children is a hope chest. Hope chests are personal private spaces to store memories and tokens of who we are. They are a place for special keepsakes and cherished items passed down or collected along their way.

As your children grow, there will be items with special meanings that you will not be able to part with. A hope chest is a wonderful place to store these cherished possessions for your children to enjoy when they become adults. They are gender-free and will stand the test of time, never made obsolete by ever-changing fads and new technology.

> **TIP!** **A hope chest is nothing more than an adult version of the child's cigar box under the bed.**

They also make great pieces of furniture. So many kinds of chests are available today, ranging from antiques, to faux finish, to contemporary. There are old steamer trunks, painted metal containers, and even shipping crates. Discount stores and catalog companies sell fabulous boxes with lids, some with locks, others without. They can double as pieces of furniture at the foot of the bed, in front of a window, as a night stand, or even as a coffee table.

> **TIP!** **Whatever style of chest you use, remember that they are *not* toys. They can be dangerous: children have suffocated inside them. Always use caution.**

To give a hope chest simply says you are expecting a bright future for your children. We have three hope chests, and they are all filling up with special collections.

Poem

Goodnight Kiss

I count it as a privilege, I count it cause for praise
To kiss my children goodnight at the close of every day.
For I know too soon they're up and gone, and walking out the door
And I'll never have a child to kiss goodnight any more.

It's very strange how times have changed
From the present to the past.
When did they grow up so quickly, the time has flown so fast.

For it seems like only yesterday I helped him with his shirt,
Or pat my baby on the back, or kiss away a hurt.
Tell a story, read a book, wipe a nose, or tie a shoe.
They never ask me to rub their backs the way they used to do.

Once it was a bother, just a troublesome kind of chore.
But now I would give anything to do it just once more.
Mommy, bounce me on your knee
Daddy flip me in the air.
Throw a rubber ball to me and help me comb my hair.

Mommy, tickle my tummy...
Daddy hold me high.
Let's go outside, for a while, or make a kite to fly...

I count it as a privilege
I count it cause for praise
To kiss my children goodnight at the close of every day

For I know too soon they're up and gone
And walking out the door
And I'll never have a child to kiss Goodnight anymore!

—Author Unknown

Chapter Fourteen

Where to Turn for Information and Support

Recommended Reading

TWINS Magazine—The Magazine for Parents of Multiples
(888) 55-TWINS
www.TWINSMagazine.com
E-mail: TWINS.editor@businessword.com

Toddlers Together: *The Complete Planning Guide for a Toddler Curriculum* by Cynthia Catlin. Gryphon House Publishing, 1994
(Volume 2 published in 1996).
A wonderful collection of "286 activities and ideas that are right for them."

Don't Sweat the Small Stuff… and It's All Small Stuff: *Simple Ways to Keep the Little Things from Taking over Your Life* by Richard Carlson, Ph.D. Hyperion, 1997.

Time-Out for Toddlers: *Positive Solutions to Typical Problems in Children* by Dr. James W. Varni and Donna G. Corwin. The Berkley Publishing Group, 1991.

Solve Your Child's Sleep Problems by Dr. Richard Ferber. Simon & Schuster, 1986.

Flicka, Ricka, Dicka and the... and *Snip Snap, Snurr and the...* are a wonderful series of twelve children's books about three little girls and three little boys who look very much alike. Written by Swedish author-artist, Maj Lindman, these books were originally published in the United States between 1932 and 1970 by Albert Whitman & Co.

Flicka, Ricka, Dicka...
and The Three Little Kittens
and The Strawberries
and The New Dotted Dresses
and The Big Red Hen
and The Little Dog
and Their New Friend
Bake A Cake

Snip, Snap, Snurr...
and The Buttered Bread
and The Red Shoes
and The Gingerbread
and The Reindeer
and The Yellow Sled
and The Big Surprise
Learn To Swim

Triplet Trouble and the... is a series of seven books about a mixed set of triplets by Debbie Dadey and Marcia Thornton Jones published by Little Apple.

Triplet Trouble...
and The Field Day Disaster
and The Runaway Reindeer
and The Talent Show Mess
and The Red Heart Race
and The Cookie Contest
and The Class Trip
and The Pizza Party

The Premature Baby Book: *A Parent's Guide to Coping and Caring in the First Years* by Helen Harrison and Ann Kositsky, R.N. St. Martin's Press, 1983.

Newborn Intensive Care: *What Every Parent Needs to Know* by Jeanette Zaichkin, RCN, MN (Editor). NICU INK Publishers, 1996.

When Pregnancy Isn't Perfect: *A Layperson's Guide to Complications in Pregnancy* by Laurie A. Rich. Larata Press, 1996.

Don't Miss Out: The Ambitious Student's Guide to Financial Aid by Anna and Robert Leider, (23rd edition), published by Octameron Associates. It explains the various forms of aid and has worksheets to help determine what your expected family contribution should be, based on the most recent programs available today. There is even software designed to run "what if" models with your expected family contribution. Much of this type of information can be ordered by writing to:

Octameron
P.O. Box 2748
Alexandria, VA 22301
(703) 836-5480
www.octameron.com

Peterson's College Money Handbook by Peterson's Guides. Published annually.

Exceptional Pregnancies—A Survival Guide to Parents Expecting Twins and *Exceptional Pregnancies—A Survival Guide to Parents Expecting Triplets or More*, both by Janet Bleyl and Katherine S. Birch, were published by The Triplet Connection. To order, please contact The Triplet Connection, P.O. Box 99571, Stockton, CA 95209, (209) 474-0885.

Support

U.S. Department of Labor, Wage and Hour Division
    Information Line
Information on The Family Leave Act of 1993
Hotline: (800) 959-3652

Mothers of Supertwins
MOST
P.O. Box 951
Brentwood, NY 11717-0627
(516) 859-1110
www.mostonline.org

NOMOTC
National Organization of Mothers of Twins Club, Inc.
P.O. Box 23188
Albuquerque, NM 87192
(800) 243-2276
www.nomotc.org
E-mail: www.nomotc@aol.com

The Triplet Connection
P.O. Box 99571
Stockton, CA 95209
(209) 474-0885
www.tripletconnection.org

La Leche League International (LLLI)
1400 N. Meacham Road
P.O. Box 4079
Schaumburg, IL 60173-4048
(847) 519-7730
www.lalecheleague.org/

Mail Order for Multiples

More Than One—A catalog for families with more than one. Features specialized products including strollers, joggers, nursing aids, hands-free bottles, accessories, and much more. Call for a free catalog.
(800) 338-TWIN
www.morethan1.com

Mainly Multiples—(a subsidiary of More Than One) A catalog filled with clever and creative cards for birth announcements, christenings, birthdays, and holidays designed for multiples. It also features customized holiday ornaments, T-shirts, and mugs. Call for a free catalog.
(800) 338-TWIN
www.morethan1.com

Tres Bambino—offers adorable and affordable custom-made children's furniture and gifts. Each piece is hand-painted and personalized with each child's name and available in eighteen different motifs. They can even custom match the décor of your kids room. Each piece is "kid-proof" not to slam or pinch little fingers and are covered in lead-free finishes. Discounts are available for twins, triplets, and quads! Call for free catalog.
(800) 501-0386

Premieware—specifically designed clothing for premature infants.
(800) 992-8469

The Wagner Stroller Blanket—These soft, fleecy, colorful, sporty blankets are customized and made to order. Tuck your babies in their strollers or car seats and travel in style with these soft sporty blankets. Call for a free catalog.
(440) 247-0170

One Step Ahead Catalog—features twin, triplet, and quadruplet baby bouncers and other baby products.
(800) 274-8440

The Triplet Connection Cookbook—is full of the best recipes submitted by the busiest moms in the world—moms of multiples! Over 400 recipes and survival tips! All profits from the sale of the book will will be donated to The Triplet Connection. To order simply send $10.00 ($8.00 each for two or more) to:
The Triplet Connection Cookbook
1771 N.W. Utah Ave.
Roseburg, OR 97470

The MaxiMom—is a hand-crafted, versatile baby carrier that is made to carry a single baby, twins, or triplets all at the same time.
(800) 643-6870

Multiple's Choice—offers a personalized storybook about your children, entitled *Love Two Times* (for twins) and *Love Three Times* (for triplets). These colorful customized books take your

own personal information and blend it into an original heart-warming story about life with your multiples. The personalized dedication page makes a special gift page for grandparents or any family member.
(800) 874-1426

Sources

Ameritech Tetherless
Ultra RangeMax Cordless Tetherless Phone
www.ameritech.com

Baby's Away—Offers everything from cribs, to rocking chairs, to swings—and even VCRs—while you and your babies are away from home. Serving most major cities and vacation destinations, *Baby's Away* offers convenient delivery and pick-up.
(800) 984-9030

The Bombay Company—"The Memory Box"
(800) 829-7789
www.bombayco.com

Eureka "The Boss" LITE Cordless Sweeper
Hacienda Vacuum & Sewing Center
15534 Gale Ave.
Hacienda Heights, CA 91745
(626) 330-1697

National Events

Annual Triplet Convention
(209) 474-0885

Twins Day Festival—takes place in a small town named by identical twin brothers, Aaron and Moses Wilcox, who settled there in

1817. Over three thousand sets of identical and fraternal twins, triplets, quads, and more attend and celebrate during the first full weekend in August in Twinsburg, Ohio.
Twins Day Festival Committee
P.O. Box 29
Twinsburg, Ohio 44807
(330) 425-3652
www.twinsday.com

Index

A

abdominoplasty, 216, 217
advice, unwanted, 13–14
airplane travel (*see* travel by plane)
airports, play areas in, 188
alone time, 173–175
Ambesol, 34
Ameritech cordless telephone, 41, 230
Ameritech Privacy Manager, 104
answering machines, 104
Arquest, 28
assisted reproduction (*see* fertility treatments)

B

babies, mixing up, 98, 99
baby blues (*see* postpartum blues)
Baby Catalogue of America, 204
baby foods, 72–73, 100, 131
baby-proofing
    baths, 149
    tips for, 93, 94, 96–97
    while travelling, 192
Baby's Away rentals, 190, 230
Baby's First Calendar, 157
baby showers
    diaper drives, 38–39
    gifts to ask for, 36–37, 39, 41–43

prepared meals, 40
registering for gifts, 35
babysitters (*see also* child care; hired help)
    and time for parents, 167
    while shopping, 179, 210
    while travelling, 188
babysitting exchanges, 173
baby wipe containers, 102
baby wipes, homemade, 128–129
backpacks, 100
bassinets, 67
baths, 148–150, 161, 201, 202
bedrest, 14, 15–20, 103
beds, 150–152, 206
bedtime rituals, 152
Beechnut, 28
binky (*see* pacifiers)
birthday cakes, 195, 197–198
birthday parties, 195, 196, 199
blood volume during pregnancy, 6
Bombay Company, 230
bookmarks, 212
books (*see* reading)
boredom during pregnancy, 15
bottle feeding, 70–72
bottles, 26, 37–38, 71
bottle warmers, 65, 76

FEB 0 9 2000